[A] PINK PEPLUM ***

Materials: 175(200,250,275)g DK yarn: oddments DK in contrasting colours for flowers: 4.50mm and 5.00mm crochet hooks.

Size: *To fit chest:* 51(56,61,66)cm [20(22,24,26)in]
Actual size: 56(61,66,71)cm [22(24,26,28)in]
Sleeve seam: 22(27,32,32)cm [8½(10½,12½, 12.½)in]
Back length: [incl peplum] 32(37,42,42)cm [12½(14½,16½, 16½)in]

Tension: 8sts and 5 rows to 5cm (2in) worked over first 5 rows of patt on 5.00mm hook.

Abbreviations: See page 37

BACK
With 5.00mm hook, make 45(49,53,57)ch.
Row 1: [RS] 1dc in 3rd ch from hook, 1dc in each ch to end, 3ch, turn.
Row 2: *miss 1st, 1tr, 1tr in missed st going behind last tr, rep from * to last st, 1tr, 3ch, turn.
Rep last row twice, 1ch, turn.
Row 5: dc to end, 3ch, turn.
Rep last 4 rows until work measures approx 25(30,35,35)cm [10(12,14,14)in] or to length required, ending with dc row. Fasten off.

FRONT
Work as for back to last 2 rows. Divide for neck shaping.
FIRST SIDE
Row 1: patt over 9(11,11,13)sts, 1tr, 1ch, turn.
Row 2: dc to end. Fasten off.
SECOND SIDE
Row 1: miss 24(24,28,28)sts, 1dc, 2ch (counts as first st), patt to end, 1ch, turn.
Row 2: dc to end. Fasten off.
With RS tog, join shoulder seams.

PEPLUM [back and front alike]
Foundation Row: With RS facing and 5.00mm hook work 2dc in each st to end, 3ch, turn.
UNDER FRILL
Row 1: work in front loops only, tr to end, 3ch, turn.
Row 2: tr as normal to end, 3ch, turn.
Row 3: tr to end, 1ch, turn.
Row 4: dc to end, 1ch, turn.
Row 5: 1dc, *2ch, 2ch, 1dc, 1ch, turn.
Row 6: *1dc, 1p, 1
Fasten off.

UPPER FRILL
With 5.00mm hook and RS facing, return to foundation row of peplum and work in rem back loops.
Row 1: 3ch, tr in back loops only to end, 1ch, turn.
Row 2: rep rows 5 & 6 of under frill once. Fasten off.

SLEEVES
With 5.00mm hook, make 41ch.
Row 1: [RS], 1dc in 3rd ch from hook, 1dc in each ch to end, 3ch, turn.   Work rows 2-5 incl as back.
Rep row 5 twice.
Rows 2-7 above form patt. Cont in patt until work measures 18(23,28,28)cm [7(9,11,11)in] or to length required. Fasten off. Mark centre st on last row of sleeve

CUFFS
Row 1: With 4.50mm hook and RS facing join yarn to first st of foundation ch of sleeve, 8ch, 1dc in 3rd ch from hook, dc to end, ss to sleeve, ss in next ch, turn.
Row 2: miss 2sts, ss in back loops to end, turn. [7sts]
Row 3: 7ss in back loops, ss to sleeve, ss in next ch, turn. Rep last 2 rows to end of sleeve.   Fasten off.

SLEEVE EDGE
Row 1: With 4.50mm hook and WS facing. 1dc, *2ch, 1dc in next ridge, rep from * to end, 1ch, turn.
Row 2: *1dc, 1p, 1dc in chsp, rep from * to end. Fasten off. Join sleeves to body by matching marked st on sleeve to shoulder seam with RS tog.

NECK EDGE
With 5.00mm hook and RS facing, join yarn to shoulder, 1ch, crab st to end, ss to join. Fasten off.
With RS tog, join sleeve and side seams.

FLOWERS [make 24]
Rnd 1: With any colour and 4.50mm hook, make 3ch. 1tr 2ch 1ss in 3rd ch from hook, *2ch 1tr 2ch 1ss in same place, rep from * 4 times [6 petals]. Fasten off.

ATTACH FLOWERS
With M, attach 10 flowers to each sleeve by tying with a knot and placing the knots to the front of the work to create a stamen effect. Attach 4 flowers to front neck.

[B] BODYWARMER, BERET and BAG **

Materials : *Bodywarmer:* 225(225,250,300)g Chunky yarn; *Beret:* 75(100,100)g; *Bag:* 75g: 6.00mm and 7.00mm hooks: 6 (7,7) buttons.

Size: *to fit chest:* 61(66,71,76)cm [24(26,28,30)in];
Actual size: 71(76,81,86)cm [28(30,32,34)in]
Back length: 32(36,36,40)cm [12½(14,14,15½)in]
Beret sizes: small/medium/large

Tension: 5sts and 3 rows = 5cm (2in) worked over patt on 7.00mm hook

Abbreviations: See page 37
NB: All Popcorns are worked on RS facing rows.

BODYWARMER
BODY [worked in one piece to armhole].
With 7.00mm hook, make 66(71,76,81)ch.

Row 1: 1tr in 4th ch from hook, 1tr in each ch to end, 3ch, turn [64(69,74,79)sts]
Row 2: [RS], 3(3,4,4)tr, *1RtrF, 1tr, 1P, 1tr, 1RtrF**, 20(23,24, 27)tr, rep from *to**once, 21(23,25, 27)tr, rep from * to ** once, tr to end, 3ch, turn.
Row 3: 3(3,4,4)tr, *RtrB, 3tr, RtrB,** 21 (23,25, 27)tr, rep from *to** once, 20(23, 24,27)tr, rep from *to** once, tr to end, 3ch, turn.
Rows 2 & 3 form patt. Cont in patt until 9 (11,11, 13)rows in all have been worked ending with WS row or for length required.   Divide for armholes
RIGHT FRONT
Row 1: patt over 14(15,16,17)sts, 3ch, turn.
Row 2: tr2tog, patt to end, 3ch, turn.
Row 3: patt to end, 3ch, turn.
Rep last row 3(3,5,5) times, ending with WS row.

Shape neck
Row 1: ss over 4sts and into 5th st, 3ch, patt to end, 3ch, turn.
Row 2: patt to end. Fasten off
BACK
Row 1: With RS facing miss next 2(3,3,4)sts, patt 31(33,35,37)sts, 3ch, turn.
Row 2: tr2tog, patt to last 3sts, tr2tog,1tr,3ch, turn.
Work a further 6(6,8,8) rows in patt. Fasten off.
LEFT FRONT
Row 1: miss next 3(3,4,4)sts, patt to end, 3ch, turn.
Row 2: patt to last 3sts, tr2tog, 1tr, 3ch, turn.
Row 3: patt to end, 3ch, turn.
Rep row 3 3(3,5,5) times.
Shape Neck
Row 1: patt to last 4sts, 3ch, turn.
Row 2: patt to end. Fasten off.
With RS tog join shoulder seams.

BANDS
RIGHT FRONT
Row 1: RS facing and 6.00mm hook, join yarn to lower R front, work dc evenly up to neck edge, turn.
NB: See page 000 for dc bands into treble rows.
Row 2: ss in back loops to end, turn.
Rep last row twice. Mark position of 6(7,7) buttons.
Row 5: [buttonhole row], *ss in back loops to marker, 1ch, miss 1st, rep from * to end, turn. Do not turn.
Row 6: Crab st in each st to end. Fasten off.
LEFT FRONT
Row 1: With 6.00mm hook and RS facing, join yarn to left front neck at centre front, work 2dc in each row end to lower edge, turn.
Rows 2-5 incl: ss in back loops to end. Fasten off.
Last Row: With 6.00mm hook and RS facing, join yarn to top edge of right band, 3dc along edge of bands, 1dc in each st and dc evenly along row ends missing 1st at shoulder seams, dc along front bands and neck edge. Do not turn, 1ch.
Crab st in each st round the garment omitting right front, ss to join. Fasten off.
ARMHOLE EDGE
Row 1: With 6.00mm hook and RS facing, join yarn to underarm seam. dc evenly all round, ss to join, 1ch. Do not turn.
Row 2: crab st all round, ss to join. Fasten off.
TO COMPLETE
Sew on buttons to correspond with buttonholes.

BAG
NB: WS of fabric is RS of work. Work in cont rnds unless otherwise stated.
Rnd 1: With 7.00mm hook, make 2ch, 8dc in 2nd ch from hook. Do not join.
Rnd 2: 2dc in each st to end. [16sts]
Rnd 3:*dc, 2dc in next st, rep from*to end. [24sts]
Rnd 4:*2dc, 2dc in next st, rep from*to end [32sts]
Rnd 5:*3dc, 2dc in next st, rep from*to end. [40sts]
Rnd 6: 40dc.   Rep row 6 9 times, ss to join, 1ch.
Rnd 16: dc, *1ch, miss 1st, dc, rep from * to end, ss to join.

Rnd 17: ss in next chsp, 3ch, tr in same sp, *2tr in chsp, rep from * to end, ss to top of 3ch to join, 1ch.
Rnd 18: crab st to end, ss to join. Fasten off.
TO COMPLETE
Make a 20in length of double twisted cord and thread through loops made on rnd 16. Knot ends of cord together.

BERET
NB: WS of fabric is RS of work. Do not join work throughout, but work in continuous rounds unless otherwise stated.
All Sizes: With 7.00mm hook, make 2ch, 10dc in 2nd ch from hook.
Rnd 2: 2dc in each st to end. [20sts]
Rnd 3: *1dc, 2dc in next st, rep from * to end.
Rnd 4: *2dc, 2dc in next st, rep from * to end.
Rnd 5: *3dc, 2dc in next st, rep from * to end.
Rnd 6: *4dc, 2dc in next st, rep from * to end.
Rnd 7: *5dc, 2dc in next st, rep from * to end.
Rnd 8: *6dc, 2dc in next st, rep from * to end.
Small Size Only
Rnds 9 & 10: dc in each st to end.
Rnd 11: dc2tog, *5dc, (dc2tog)twice, rep from * to last 6sts, 4dc, dc2tog.
Rnd 12:*dc2tog, 3dc, rep from*to last 2sts, dc2tog.
Rnds 13 & 14: *2dc, dc2tog to last st, 1dc, ss in next st of last row, turn. Do not fasten off.
Medium Size Only
Rnd 9: *7dc, 2dc in next st, rep from * to end.
Rnd 10: 4dc, 2dc in next st, *8dc, 2dc in next st, rep from * to last 4sts, 4dc.
Rnd 11: dc2tog, *6dc, (dc2tog)twice, rep from * to last 2sts, dc2tog.
Rnd 12: *dc2tog, 4dc, rep from * to end.
Rnd 13: *3dc, dc2tog, rep from * to last st, 1dc.
Rnds 14 & 15: *2dc, dc2tog, rep from * to last st, 1dc, ss in next st of last row, turn. Do not fasten off.
Large Size Only
Rnd 9: *7dc, 2dc in next st, rep from * to end.
Rnd 10: 4dc, 2dc in next st, *8dc, 2dc in next st, rep from * to last 4sts, 4dc.
Rnd 11: 5dc, 2dc in next st, *9dc, 2dc in next st, rep from * to last 4sts, 4dc.
Rnds 12 & 13: dc in each st to end.
Rnd 14: dc2tog, *5dc, dc2tog, rep from * to last 3sts, 3dc.
Rnd 15: *3dc, dc2tog, rep from * to last 4sts, 4dc.
Rnd 16 & 17:*3dc, dc2tog, rep from*to last st, 1dc.
Rnd 18: 3dc, *dc2tog, 3dc, rep from*to last st, 1ss.
Do not fasten off.
BAND · All Sizes
Row 1: With 6.00mm hook make 5ch, ss in 2nd ch from hook and each ch, ss in next dc on beret, turn.
Row 2: miss last ss, ss in back loops to end, 1ch, turn.
Row 3: ss in back loop of each st, ss in next dc, turn.
Rep rows 2 & 3 until band is complete. Fasten off.
TO COMPLETE
Join band seam. Make tassel or pom-pom and sew to centre of beret.

[C] SPRINGTIME ★★★★

Materials: 175(200,200)g DK yarn: oddments of DK in the following colours: green, white, orange, yellow for grass and flowers, brown for mouse, 4.00mm, 5.00mm, & 5.50mm hooks, 2 buttons (shoulder opening), ladybird button, 2 small beads (mouse eyes).

Size: *To fit chest* 46(51,55)cm [18(20,22)in]
Actual chest: 56(61,66)cm [22(24,26)in]
Back length: 35(39,39)cm [14(15½,15½)in] inc frill.
Sleeve seam: 17(20,24)cm [6½(8,9½)in]

Tension: 14sts and 17 rows worked over patt on 5.50mm hook to 10cm [4in]

Abbreviations: See page 37

BACK
[NB: Garment is worked from side to side]
With 5.50mm hook, make 43(49,49)ch.
Row 1: 1dc in 3rd ch from hook, 1dc in each ch to end, 1ch, turn.
Row 2: [RS] dc in back loops only to end, 1ch, turn.
Rep row 2 44(54,64)times. Fasten off.

FRONT
Work as for back for 16(20, 24)rows.
Divide for neck opening, working in back loops only..
FIRST SIDE
Row 1: ss over 6sts, 1ss 1ch 1dc in next st, dc to end, 1ch, turn.
Row 2: dc to end, 1ch, turn. Rep row 2 12(14,16) times. Add 8ch, to last row, turn.
SECOND SIDE
Row 1: dc in 3rd ch from hook, dc in each ch, dc to end, 1ch, turn.
Row 2: dc to end, 1ch, turn. Rep last row 14(18, 22)times more. Fasten off.

LOWER EDGING AND FRILL (front and back alike)
With 5.00mm hook and RS facing, join yarn to first row end at lower edge. Work dc as normal.
Size 1: 1dc,1dc in next row end,*miss 1 row end,1dc in next 2 row ends,rep from*to end. Fasten off(31sts)
Size 2:1dc,1dc in next row end,*miss 1 row end, 1dc in next 2 row ends,rep from*to end. Fasten off(38sts)
Size 3: 1dc, 1dc in next row end, *miss 1 row end, 1dc in next 2 row ends, rep from * to last row end, 1dc in last row end. Fasten off. (45sts). Join in green with ss.

All sizes
Row 2: 1ch 1dc in first st. To create a 'grass' effect along this row, work spike sts of differing lengths into body of garment to end, 1ch, turn (see illustration).
Row 3: dc to end, turn. Fasten off green. Join in main colour, 3ch.

Size 1: **Row 4:** 2tr in same st as 3ch, (2tr in next st)twice, *1tr, 2tr in next st, rep from * to last 2sts, 2tr in next st)twice, 1ch, turn.

Size 2: **Row 4:** 2tr in same st as 3ch, (2tr in next st)twice, *1tr, 2tr in next st, rep from * to last st, 2tr, 1ch, turn.

Size 3: **Row 4:** 1tr in same st as 3ch, 1tr, 2tr in next st, rep from * to end, 1ch, turn.

Sizes 1 & 2: **Row 5:** 2dc, *1dc 5ch 1dc in next st, 4dc, rep from * to last 2sts, 2dc, 1ch, turn. [10(12) 5ch loops].

Size 3: **Row 5:** 3dc, *1dc 5ch 1dc in next st, 4dc, rep from * to end, 1ch, turn. (13 5ch loops)

All sizes: **Row 6:** ss in each dc, *ss in 5ch loop, (2ch 2tr 2ch 1ss into next loop)3 times, miss next dc, 4ss, miss next dc, rep from * to end, ss in rem dc. Fasten off.

SLEEVES
NB: Sleeve is worked from side to side
With 5.50mm hook make 23(29,35)ch.
Row 1: [WS] 1dc in 3rd ch from hook, dc to end, 1ch, turn.
Row 2: dc in back loops only to end, 1ch, turn.
Rep last row 34 times. Fasten off.

SLEEVE FRILL
With 5.00 hook, join yarn to first st of first row end with a ss.
Row 1: [RS] 1dc in same st [cont to work along edge of rows], 1dc,*miss next row end, 1dc in next 2 row ends, rep from * to end, ss in last st, 1ch, turn.
Row 2: 2dc *1dc 5ch 1dc in next st, 4dc, rep from * to last st, 1dc in last st, 1ch, turn.
Row 3: miss first st, 1ss *1ss into 5ch loop, (2ch2tr 2ch1ss into next loop)3 times, miss next st, 4dc, miss next st, rep from * to last 2sts, 2ss. Fasten off.
With RS tog join left shoulder seam.

NECK AND SHOULDER EDGING
With 5.00mm hook and RS facing, join yarn to first st on back, (shoulder edge) 1dc in same st, dc in next row end, *miss next row end, 1dc in each of next 2 row ends, rep from * across back to shoulder seam. Do not turn. Cont to work 5dc evenly down left front, 11(13,15)dc across front neck opening and 5dc up right front, 1dc 1ch 1dc in same st as last dc, **miss 1 row end, dc in next 2 row ends,rep from ** to end, 1ch, turn. Mark position for 2 buttonholes.
Row 2: (buttonhole row) work along shoulder only, *dc to marker, 2ch, miss 1dc, rep from * to end, 1ch, turn.
Row 3: 1dc in each dc and chsp to end, 1ch, do not turn.
Row 4: Crab st all around neck and shoulder edgings. Fasten off.

FLOWERS [make 13]
With 5.00mm hook and contrasting yarn, make 3ch, 1tr 2ch 1ss in 3rd ch from hook, * 2ch 1tr 2ch 1ss in same place, rep from * 3 times. [5 petals] Fasten off.

MOUSE
Make a 9cm [3½in] single twisted cord for tail and set aside.   [NB: WS of fabric is RS]
Rnd 1: With 4.00mm hook and brown yarn, make 3ch, 8dc in 3rd ch from hook, do not join.
Rnd 2: Work in cont rnds, 18dc.
Make a very large knot at the body end of tail, slip through centre 'ring' at end of mouse.
Rnd 3: (dc2tog, 1dc) twice, (dc2tog) 5 times. Fasten off.
Mouse ears: With 4.00mm hook and brown, make 3ch, 1dc 3tr 1ss in 2nd ch from hook, rep in last ch. Fasten off.

TO COMPLETE
Overlap buttonhole band at shoulder edge, over first few sts of back and sew in place.
Mark centre st on last row of sleeve and match to shoulder seam. Sew in sleeves easing to fit.
Using contrasting yarn, attach flowers to front, back and 2 to each sleeve, knotting flowers at front of work to create a stamen effect.
Sew ears to mouse a short way from point of nose.
Sew on 2 small beads for eyes.
Sew mouse to front of garment just above frill.
Sew ladybird button to front just above frill.
Sew on buttons to correspond with buttonholes.
With RS tog join side and underarm seams.

[D] I LOVE MY TEDDY...BARE ***

Materials: DK yarn - 150(175,200,225)g in M, 50(50,50, 50)g in yellow (A), 25(25,25,25)g in red (B), oddment of white (C): 4.00mm,4.50mm, 5.00mm crochet hooks.

Size: *To fit chest:* 56(61,66,71)cm [22(24, 26,28)in]
Actual chest size: 61(66,71,76)cm [24(26, 28,30)in]
Back length: 38(38,39,39)cm [15(15,15½,15½)in]
Sleeve seam: 23(26,29,32)cm [9(10¼,11½,12¾)in]

Tension: 8sts and 9 rows to 5cm [2in] worked over patt on 5.00mm hook.

Abbreviations: See page37

FRONT

With 5.00mm hook and M, make 46(50,54,58)ch.
Row 1:1dc in 2nd ch from hook, dc to end,1ch, turn.
Row 2: sdc to end, 1ch, turn.
Row 3: cont by following chart on pg 6 for colour changes and neck shaping. Fasten off.

BACK

Work as for front for first 2 rows. Follow chart [pg 6] for colour changes. Fasten off. Join shoulder seams.

SLEEVES

With 5.00mm hook, make 28ch.
Row 1: 1dc in 3rd ch from hook, dc to end,1ch,turn.
Row 2: Follow chart using sdc. Inc 1st at each end of rows 3, 7, and every following 6th row, until sleeve measures 19(22, 25,28)cm [7½(8½,10,11)in] or to length required. Fasten off.

CUFFS

With 4.00mm hook join M to first st of sleeve.
Row 1: 3ch,tr to end, join in A, 2ch, turn.
Row 2: 1RtrB, *1RtrF, 1RtrB, rep from * to last st, 1htr, join in M, 2ch, turn.

Row 3: 1RtrF, *1RtrB, 1RtrF, rep from * to last st, 1htr, join in B, 2ch, turn.
Row 4: As row 2, join in M.
Row 5: As row 3.   Fasten off.

WELTS

With 4.50mm hook join M to base and work as cuff.

NECK EDGE

With 4.50 hook join M to shoulder seam, 1ch, crab st around neck, ss to join. Fasten off.

TEDDY

EARS [2 alike]: With 5.00mm hook and A, make 4ch commencing with a slip knot that tightens from the tail end.
Row 1: 10tr in 4th ch from hook,1ch,turn.
Row 2: (3dc,2dc in next st)twice, dc to end, 1ch, do not turn. Work 1 row crab st. Fasten off.
Sew ears to sides of head.
EYES [alike]: With 4.50mm hook and M, make 2ch, 9dc in 2nd ch from hook, ss to join. Fasten off.
SNOUT: With A, make a 5cm [2in] diameter pompom and sew centrally to lower half of face.
NOSE: With 5.00mm hook and M, make 3ch, tr6tog in 3rd ch from hook. Fasten off.

ASSEMBLING FACE

Sew nose centrally to upper half of snout.
Sew eyes to face directly above snout.
Using white yarn embroider eye feature.
With M embroider tummy button.

TO COMPLETE

With WS tog, put centre of last row of sleeve to shoulder seam. Sew in sleeves, easing to fit. Join sleeve and side seams in one.

[E] DOLLY MIXTURE **
[Cardigan & Beret]

Materials: *Cardigan:* 250(250,300,350)g Aran yarn in M, 100(100,100,100)g Aran yarn in C. *Beret:* 50g M, 25g C: 5.00mm and 5.55mm crochet hooks: 6(6,7,7) buttons,

Size: *To fit chest:* 61(66,71,76)cm [24(26,28,30)in]
Actual size: 71(76,81,87)cm [28(30,32,34)in]
Back length: 34(37,40,43)cm [13½(14½,15¾,17)in]
Sleeve length: 22(25,29,33)cm [8½(10,11½,13)in]

Tension: 6dc and 5 rows to 5cm [2in].

Abbreviations: See page 37

CARDIGAN

BODY [worked in one to armholes]

With 5.50mm hook and M work [85(91,97,103)ch]
Row 1: [RS] 1dc in 3rd ch from hook, dc to end, 1ch, turn.
Row 2: dc to end,1ch, turn [84(90,96,102)sts].
Rep row 2   11 times.

Row 14:[pocket opening]5(5,6,6)dc, 12ch, miss 12sts, 50(56,60,66)dc,12ch,miss 12sts, 5(5,6,6)dc,1ch,turn
Row 15: dc to end, 1ch, turn. [84(90,96,102)sts].
Row 16: as row 2.   Rep row 2 until work measures 18 (21,24,27)cm [7(8,9½,10½)in] or length required. Divide for armholes.

RIGHT FRONT

Row 1: RS is facing, work 21(22,24,25)dc, 1ch, turn. Place marker at beg of this row
Row 2: dc to end, 1ch, turn.
Work 2 rows more on these 21(22,24,25)sts, 1ch, turn
Row 5: dc2tog, dc to end, 1ch, turn.
Row 6: dc to end, 1ch, turn.
Rep rows 5 & 6 5times.
Rep row 5 once more. Fasten off.

BACK

With RS facing rejoin yarn to next st, 1ch,
42(46,48,52)dc, 1ch, turn.
Row 2: dc to end, 1ch, turn. Rep row 2 15 times.
Fasten off.

LEFT FRONT

With RS facing rejoin yarn to next st, 1ch, dc to end,
1ch, turn. Place a marker in end of this row.
Row 2: dc to end, 1ch, turn.
Work on these 21(22,24,25)sts for 2 rows, 1ch, turn.
Row 5: dc to last 2sts, dc2tog, 1ch, turn.
Row 6: dc to end, 1ch, turn. Rep last 2 rows 5 times.
Work row 5 once more. Fasten off.
Place RS of shoulders tog and join.

POCKET

Pocket Lining [make 2 alike]
With 5.50mm hook and M, join yarn to last of 12ch of
pocket opening, 1ch, 1dc in same place, 11dc, 1ch, turn
Row 2: dc to end, 1ch, turn. [12sts].
Work row 2 8 times. Fasten off.
Sew lining to inside of cardigan ckecking it does not pull
of shape and that the stitches do not show on the front.
Pocket Edge: With 5.00mm hook join C to first
missed st of pocket opening 1ch, 1dc in same place
11dc (check both edges are the same and if necessary
add 1 extra dc to last st). *Do not turn work.*
Row 2: 1ch, crab st to end. Fasten off.

SLEEVES

With 5.50mm hook and M make 31(31,33,33)ch.
Row 1: 1dc in 3rd ch from hook, 1dc in each ch to
end, 1ch, turn. [30(30,32,32)sts].
Row 2: dc to end, 1ch, turn.
Rep row 2 until work measures 18.5(21.5,25.5,
29.5)cm. [7¼(8½,10½,11½)in] or length required.

CUFFS

With 5.00mm hook join C to first ch of sleeve.
Row 1: 12ch, 1ss in 2nd ch from hook, ss in each ch
to end, ss into next ch on sleeve to anchor the cuff, ss in
next ch to start next row.
Row 2: miss last 2ss's made, ss in back loops of each st
to end, turn.
Row 3: ss in back loops to end, ss in next 2ch on
sleeve, turn.   Rep last 2 rows to end of starting ch on
sleeve. Fasten off.

WELT

With 5.00mm hook join C to bottom of left front.
Row 1: 7ch, ss in 2nd ch from hook, ss to end, ss into
next base ch,turn.
Row 2: miss last ss, ss into back loops to end, turn.
Row 3: ss in back loops to end, ss into next row, turn.
Rep rows 2 and 3 once.   Rep row 2 once.
Row 7: ss in back loops to end, ss into next 2 base ch,
turn.
Row 8: Miss 2 sts, ss in back loops to end, turn.
Row 9: ss in back loops to end, ss into next base ch.
Row 10: Miss 1st, ss in back loops only to end, turn.

Rep last 4 rows ending last row at lower edge of welt.
Do not fasten off but continue to make the bands.

BANDS

ss in back loop to front, ss in each row end up right
front, ss in sts at neck, ss in each row end down left
front to welt, ss in back loop of each st to end, turn.
Row 2: missing 1st at each shoulder, ss in back loops to
end, turn.
Row 3: As row 2. On the right front for a girl and left
front for a boy mark 6(6,7,7) places for buttonholes.
Row 4: [Buttonhole row] missing 1st at shoulders *ss in
back loops to first marker, 1ch, miss 1st, rep from * to
end, turn.
Row 5: *ss in back loops to 1chsp, 1ss in 1chsp, rep
from * to end, turn.
Row 6: As row 2. *Do not turn.*
Row 7: Crab st to end. Fasten off.

TO COMPLETE

Join sleeve seams with RS tog. Seam is on WS but it is a
turn back cuff so change sides of fabric for joining cuffs.
Insert sleeves into armholes checking sleeves match.
Sew on buttons to match buttonholes. Sew in ends

BERET

[Work in cont rnds as a spiral with WS of fabric as RS].
With 5.50mm hook and M make a slip knot as shown
on page 000, 2ch, 10dc in 2nd ch from hook. Do not
join but mark beg of each round.
Rnd 2: 2dc in each st to end. [20sts]
Rnd 3: *1dc, 2dc in next st, rep from * to end. [30sts]
Rnd 4: *2dc, 2dc in next st, rep from * to end. [40sts]
Rnd 5: *3dc, 2dc in next st, rep from * to end. [50sts]
Rnd 6: *4dc, 2dc in next st, rep from * to end. [60sts]
Rnd 7: *5dc, 2dc in next st, rep from * to end. [70sts]
Rnd 8: *6dc, 2dc in next st, rep from * to end. [80sts]
Rnd 9: *7dc, 2dc in next st, rep from * to end. [90sts]
Rnd 10:*8dc, 2dc in next st, rep from*to end [100sts]
Rnd 11:*9dc, 2dc in next st, rep from*to end [110sts]
Rnd 12: 1dc in each st.
Rnd 13: dc2tog *7dc, (dc2tog)twice, rep from * to
last 9sts, 7dc, dc2tog.
Rnd 14: *5dc, (dc2tog)twice, rep from * to end.
Rnd 15: *3dc, dc2tog, rep from * to end.
Rnd 16: *2dc, dc2tog, rep from * to end, ss in next st.
Fasten off.

HAT BAND

With 5.00mm hook and C join to last st with 1ss.
Make 7ch.
Row 1: ss in 2nd ch from hook, ss to end, ss in next st
on beret, turn.
Row 2: miss last st, ss in back loops to end, turn.
Row 3: ss in back loops to end, ss in next st on beret,
turn.
Rep last two rows round beret.
Sew seam of band.
Make tassel or pompom and sew to centre of beret.

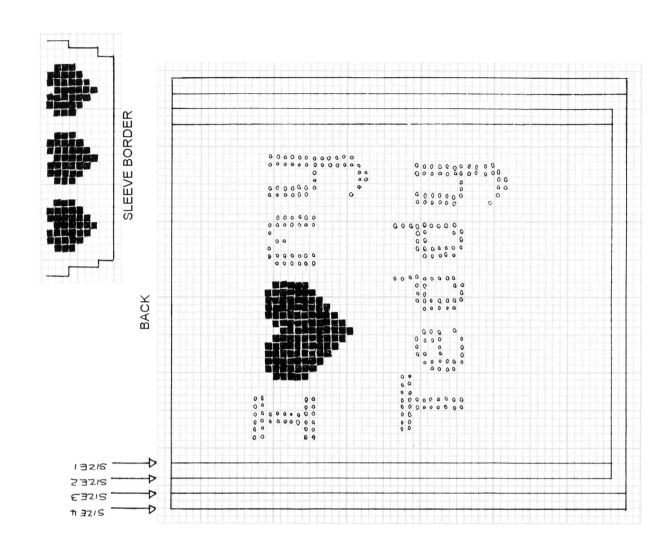

I LOVE MY TEDDY

SLEEVE BORDER

BACK

○ yellow
■ red
□ black

SIZE 1
SIZE 2
SIZE 3
SIZE 4

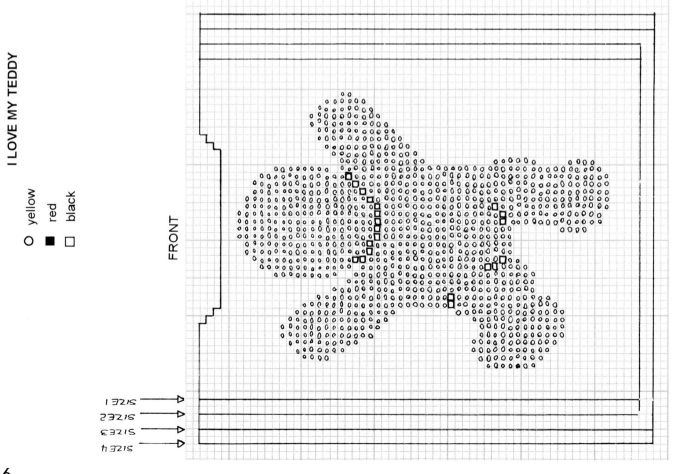

FRONT

SIZE 1
SIZE 2
SIZE 3
SIZE 4

[F] ZIGZAG TUNIC ***

Materials: 150(200,200)g DK in M, 25(25,30)g DK in A and 25(25,30)g DK in B. 4.50mm and 5.00mm crochet hooks.

Size: *To fit chest:* 56(61,66)cm [22(24,26)in]
Actual size: 64(69,74)cm [25(27,29)in]
Sleeve seam: 23.5(26.5,29)cm [9¼(10½,11½)in]
Back length: 39(41,43)cm [15¼(16,17)in]

Tension: 16sts and 12 rows over patt to 11cm[4¼in] with 5.00mm hook.

Abbreviations: See page 37

NB: RS rows are worked in trebles, WS rows are worked in double crochet.

BODY

With 5.00m hook & M make 49(53,57)ch

Row 1: 1tr in 4th ch from hook,tr to end, 1ch, turn. [47(51,55)sts] NB: 1st row of border now worked.

Row 2: Follow chart 000 for colour changes, dc to end, 3ch, turn. Work 8 rem rows of border.

Row 11: tr to end, 1ch, turn.

Row 12: dc to end, 3ch ,turn.

Work 9(11,13)rows more.

YOKE - Follow chart. Fasten off.

With RS tog, join shoulder seams on WS.

COLLAR

With 4.50mm(5.00mm, 5.00mm) hook and M, join yarn to right shoulder seam with ss, make 23ch.

Row 1: 1dc in 3rd ch from hook, dc to end, ss in next st at neck, turn.

Row 2: miss last ss, ss in back loop to end, turn [22sts]

Row 3: ss in back loop of each st, ss in next row end or next st, turn. Cont in patt round neck. Join collar tog.

SLEEVES

With 5.00mm hook and M, make 29ch.

Row 1: 1tr in 4th ch from hook, tr to end, 1ch, turn [27sts] NB: 1st row of border worked.

Follow chart for a further 10 rows.

Row 12: dc to end, 3ch, turn.

Row 13: tr to end, 1ch, turn.

Rep last 2 rows without colour changes. Inc 1st each end of every 4th row, until sleeve measures 23.5(26.5, 29)cm [9¼(10½,11½)in] or length required. Place marker in centre of last row and match to shoulder seam

SLEEVE AND LOWER BODY EDGING

With RS facing, 4.50mm hook and M, crab st all round, ss to join. Fasten off.

TO COMPLETE

Insert sleeves with 5.00mm hook, M and WS tog beg at underarm, crab st to end, fasten off.

Join underarm and side seams in one with RS tog.

With A make 2tassels 12cm[4¾in] in length[see pg 000]. Attach tassels to base of each bobble by looping them through the bobble.

+ Purple
O Pink
● 1B in purple

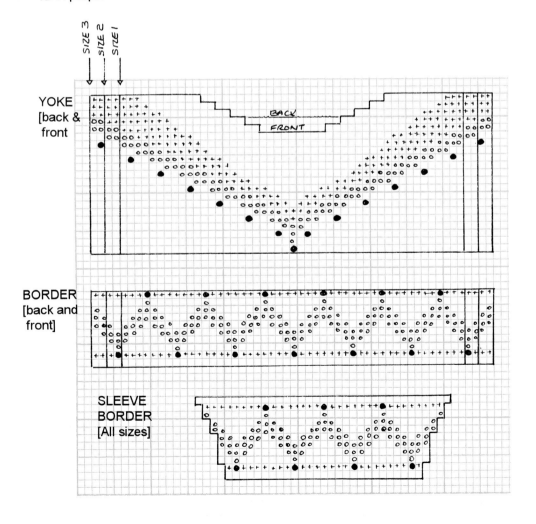

[G] KITTY CARDIGAN ****

Materials: 150(150,150)g DK yarn in M; 50(100,100)g in A; 50(50,50)g in B; oddments of green and red: 4.50mm & 5.00mm hooks; 5 buttons.

Size:
To fit chest 61-69(66-74, 71-79)cm [24-27(26-29,28-31)in]
Actual size 71(76,81)cm [28(30,32)in]
Back length 41(41,46)cm [16(16,18)in]
Sleeve seam 23(26,28)cm [9(10,11)in]

Tension: 12sts and 16 rows to 9cm (3½in) worked in patt on 5.00mm hook.

Abbreviation: See page 37

NB: Main body and sleeves (except brickwork) worked in sdc,

BACK

With 5.00mm hook and A, make 48(54,60)ch.
Row 1:[RS] 1dc in 3rd ch from hook, dc to end, 1ch, turn [47(53,59)sts].
Row 2: dc to end, 1ch, turn.
Row 3: join in B, do not fasten off A, working in front loops of sts and following chart, working ss and 'V' as appropriate. Fasten off B. Do not turn.
Row 4: pick up loop of A from row 2 and working into rem back loops of sts, dc to end, 1ch, turn.
Row 5: As row 2
Row 6: As row 3. Rows 4-6 form patt. Cont to work in patt for a total of 18(18,21)rows [see chart].
Fasten off A. Join in M and work rem of body.
Row 19(19,22): sdc in each st to end, 1ch, turn.
Rep last row, following chart for colour changes to end. Fasten off.

FRONTS

With 5.00mm hook and yarn A make 23(26,29)ch.
Row 1: 1dc in 3rd ch from hook, dc to end, 1ch, turn 22(25,28)sts. Work as for back, following both left and right fronts charts for colour changes and shaping by working a dec as dc2tog.
With RS tog join shoulder seams.

FRONT BANDS AND NECK
Row 1: With 4.50mm hook and RS facing, join A to 1st st at lower right front, 1dc in each row end and each st to end of brickwork, join in yellow and work 1dc in each row end and each st to brickwork on left front.
Join in A and work to end, turn.
Cont working in orange and yellow yarn as appropriate.
Row 2-4 incl: ss in back loops all round missing 1st at each shoulder seam, turn. Mark position of 4 buttons - (5th buttonhole will be made in welt).
Row 5: (buttonhole row), *ss in back loops to marker, 1ch, miss 1st, rep from * to end, turn.
Row 6: ss in back loops of each st and chsp to end, turn
Row 7: rep row 2, 1ch, do not turn.
Row 8: Crab st around. Fasten off. Join side seams.

WELTS
NB: Work buttonhole either 3rd row, or 3rd row from end.
With 4.50mm hook and yarn B, join to lower edge of left front with a ss, make 10ch.
Row 1: ss in 2nd ch from hook, ss to end [9sts], ss into next row end on band, turn.
Row 2: miss last st, ss in back loops to end, turn.

LEFT SLEEVE

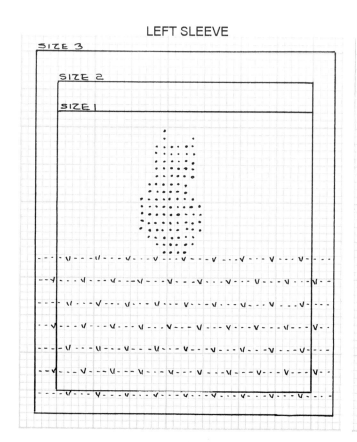

RIGHT SLEEVE

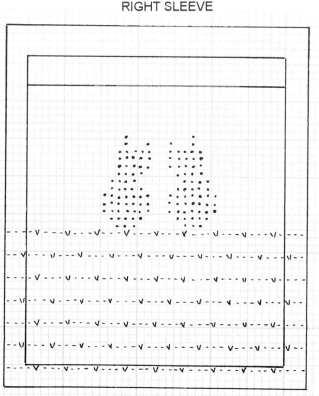

V dc spike worked into two rows previous
- ss into front loop
● black
x place marker

LEFT FRONT

RIGHT FRONT

BACK

SIZE 1
SIZE 2
SIZE 3

SIZE 1
SIZE 2
SIZE 3

9

Row 3: ss in back loops to end, ss into next row end on band, turn.
Row 4: Rep row 2
Row 5: Rep row 3
Row 6: Rep row 2
Row 7: Join in yellow and fasten off orange, ss in back loops of each st, ss into next 2ch on base, turn.
Row 8: miss 2sts, ss in back loops to end, turn.
Row 9: ss in back loops of each ss, ss in next base ch, turn.   Rows 6-9 form patt.   Cont in patt joining in orange at right front band.

SLEEVES
With 5.00mm hook and yarn A, make 36(36,42)ch.
Row 1: 1dc in 3rd ch from hook, dc to end, 1ch, turn.
Work as back following sleeve charts for colour changes. Mark centre stitch on last row of sleeve.   With WS tog, match marked stitch on sleeve with shoulder seam. Join sleeves using 5.00mm hook, yarn M and with WS facing, ease to fit and crab stitch sleeves to body.

CUFFS
With 4.50mm hook and RS facing join yarn A to first st, 8ch, turn.
Row 1: ss in 2nd ch from hook, ss to end [7sts], ss into next 2 base ch on sleeve, turn.
Row 2: miss 2ss, ss in back loops to end, turn. [7sts]
Row 3: ss in back loops to end, ss into next 2 base ch, turn.   Last 2 rows form patt.
Cont in patt to sleeve end.   Fasten off.

ADDITIONAL FEATURES
Vine [make 3 alike]
With 4.50mm hook and green yarn, make 3ch, *1tr 1 picot 2ch 1ss in 3rd ch from hook [1 leaf made], 5ch, rep from * 14 times omitting 5ch on last rep. Fasten off. [15 leaves].
Sew vine to brickwork as follows: 1 on left sleeve, 1 on right front, 1 on back [bet 2 largest cats].
Ladybird [make 2]
Body: With 4.00mm hook and red yarn make 3ch, tr6tog in 3rd ch from hook. Fasten off red.
Head: With 4.00mm hook and black yarn make 2ch, 3dc 1ss in 2nd ch from hook. Fasten off. Sew head to body. With black yarn, embroider spots to body then sew to vine at right front and left sleeve.
Neck bows for small cats only.
Cut a 15cm[6in] length of yarn. Tie to neck in a bow. With A, embroider eye detail to cat on right front.
Whiskers: With 1 strand of black yarn or embroidery thread, carefully add whisker detail.
Tails: Small cats on right sleeve and small cat on left front, make a 8cm[3in] length of double twisted cord. For rem cats make a 10cm [4in] length of quadruple twisted cord

TO COMPLETE
Sew tails in position on cats.
Join sleeve and side seams.
Sew on buttons to correspond with buttonholes.

[H] LITTLE RED RIDING HOOD ****

Materials: *Coat:* 450(550)g Aran weight yarn; *Hat:* 75(75)g Aran weight yarn: 5.00mm & 5.50mm crochet hooks: 4(5) 2.5cm [1in] dia buttons
Size : *To fit chest:* 61-71(71-81)cm [24-28(28-32)in]
Actual chest size: 71(82)cm [28(32)in]
Sleeve seam: 25(29)cm [10(11¼)in]
Back length: 46(56)cm [18(22)in]
Hat around face: 36cm [14in]
Tension: 14sts and 10 rows to 10cm [4in] worked over patt on 5.50mm hook. [Test worked in Wendy Toddler weight Aran]
Abbreviations: See page 37

COAT
BACK
With 5.50mm hook, make 51(59)ch.
Row 1: [RS] 1tr in 4th ch from hook, tr to end, 1ch, turn
Row 2: 1dc, (1dtr, 1dc)2(4)times, *1B, 7dc, 1B, 1dc, 4RtrB, 1dc, rep from * once, 1B, 7dc, 1B, 1dc, (1dtr, 1dc)2(4)times, 3ch, turn.
Row 3: 6(10)tr, *1CV, 3tr, 4RtrF, 3tr, rep from * once, 1CV, 7(11)tr, 1ch, turn.
Row 4: 2dc, (1dtr,1dc)1(3)times, 1dc, 1B*, 7dc, 1B, 1dc, 4RtrB, 1dc, 1B, rep from * once, 7dc, 1B, 2dc, (1dtr,1dc)1(3)times, 1dc, 3ch, turn.
Row 5: 6(10)tr, *1CV, 3tr, 1 twist, 3tr, rep from * once, 1CV, 7(11)tr, 1ch, turn. Rows 2-5 incl form patt.
Cont in patt until work measures 30(40)cm [12 (16)in], or length required, ending with RS row.

ARMHOLES
Row 1: ss over 4sts, 1ss 1ch 1dc in next st, patt to last 4sts, 3ch, turn.
Row 2: patt to end, 1ch, turn.
Row 3: patt to end, 3ch, turn.
Work 11 rows in patt. Fasten off.

RIGHT FRONT
With 5.50mm hook make 25(29)ch.
Row 1: 1tr in 4th ch from hook, tr to end, 1ch, turn.
Row 2: 1dc, (1dtr, 1dc)2(4)times, 1B, 7dc, 1B, 1dc, 4RtrB, 1dc, 1B, 2dc, 3ch, turn.
Row 3: 3tr, 4RtrF, 3tr, 1CV, 7(11)tr, 1ch, turn.
Row 4: 2dc, (1dtr, 1dc)1(3)times, 1dc, 1B, 7dc, 1B, 1dc, 4RtrB, 1dc, 1B, 2dc, 3ch, turn.
Row 5: 3tr, 1 twist, 3tr, 1CV, 7(11)tr, 1ch, turn.
Rows 2-5 incl form patt.
Cont in patt until work measures the same as back to armholes.

ARMHOLES
Row 1: ss over 4sts, (1ss 1ch 1dc)in next st, patt to end, 3ch, turn.
Row 2: patt to end, 1ch, turn.   Work 8 rows in patt.
Row 11: patt to last 6sts, 3ch, turn.
Row 12: patt to end, 1ch, turn. Work 2 rows in patt. Fasten off.

LEFT FRONT

With 5.50mm hook, make 25(29)ch.
Row 1: 1tr in 4th ch from hook, tr to end, 1ch, turn.
Row 2: 2dc, 1B, 1dc, 4RtrB, 1dc, 1B, 7dc, 1B, 1dc, (1dtr,1dc)2(4)times, 3ch, turn.
Row 3: 6(10)tr, 1CV, 3tr, 4RtrF, 4tr, 1ch, turn.
Row 4: 2dc, 1B, 1dc, 4RtrB, 1dc, 1B, 7dc, 1B, 2dc, (1dtr,1dc) 1(3) times, 1dc, 3ch, turn.
Row 5: 6(10)tr, 1CV, 3tr, 1 twist, 4tr, 1ch, turn.
Rows 2-5 incl form patt. Cont in patt until work measures as back to armholes.

ARMHOLES

Row 1: patt to last 4sts, turn. Work 9 rows in patt.
Row 11: ss over first 6sts, patt to end.
Work 3 rows on these sts. Fasten off.

SLEEVES

With 5.50mm hook, make 31ch.
Row 1: RS is facing, 1tr in 4th ch from hook, 1tr in each ch to end, 1ch, turn.
Row 2: 3dc, *1B, 1dc, 4RtrB, 1dc, 1B**, 7dc, rep from * to ** once, 3dc, 3ch, turn.
Row 3: 4tr, 4RtrF, 3tr, 1CV, 3tr, 4RtrF, 5tr, 1ch, turn
Row 4: 2dc in first st, 2dc,1B, *1dc, 4RtrB, 1dc, 1B, **7dc, 1B, rep from * to ** once, 2dc, 2dc in last st. [2 inc made.]
Row 5: 5tr, 1twist, 3tr, 1CV, 3tr, 1twist, 6tr, 1ch,turn
Rows 2-5 incl form patt, dc sts [indicated in bold print on row 4] will inc by 1st on every 4th row.
Cont in patt for 16 rows.
Row 17: 1CV [worked around stem of 3rd tr on row 15], 3tr, *1twist, 3tr, 1CV**, 3tr, rep from * to ** once, 1tr, 1ch, turn. Cont in patt to row 26.
Size 1: Fasten off.
Size 2: Row 26: *1dc, 1B, 7dc, 1B, 1dc**, 4RtrB, rep from * once, rep from * to ** once, 3ch, turn.
Cont in patt until sleeve measures 25(29)cm [10 (11¼)in], or length required. Fasten off.

SLEEVE EDGE

Row 1: With 5.00mm hook and RS facing join yarn to first base ch, dc to end, ss to join, 1ch, do not turn.
Row 2: crab st around, ss to join. Fasten off.
With RS tog join shoulder seams, side seams, sleeve seams. Join sleeves to armholes, easing to fit.

RIGHT FRONT BAND

Row 1: With 5.50mm hook and RS facing, join yarn to first st of right front, work 2dc in each tr row end and 1dc in each dc row end to neck, turn. [*NB:* Check at this point the band is lying flat on centre front of coat].
Row 2: ss in back loops to end, turn. Rep row 2 3 times
Mark evenly the position of 4(5) buttons.
Row 6: [buttonhole row] *2ss in back looks only to first marker, 2ch, miss 2sts, rep from * 3(4)times, ss in back loops to end, turn. [4(5) buttonholes made].
Row 7: ss in back loops of sts and into each chsp to end, turn. Rep row 2 twice. Do not turn.
Row 10: crab st to end. Fasten off.

LEFT FRONT BAND

Row 1: With 5.50mm hook and RS facing, join to first st on left front at neck edge, work 2dc in each tr row end and 1dc in each dc row end to lower edge, turn.
Row 2: ss in back loops to end, turn.
Rep row 2 7 times, 1ch. Do not turn.

Row 10: crab st to end. Fasten off.

UPPER COLLAR

Row 1: With 5.00mm hook and RS facing, join yarn to first st of right front after band, 11dc to shoulder, 16dc along back, 11dc down left front [excl band],1ch, turn.
Row 2: using front loop of sts only, 1dc, 2dc in next st, *2dc, 2dc in next st, rep from * to end, 1ch, turn.
Row 3: dc to end, 1ch, turn.
Row 4: miss first st, 3dc, *2dc in next st, 3dc, rep from * to last 3sts, 3dc, turn.
Row 5: miss 1st,1dc,1B, dc to last 3sts,1B,dc2tog, turn.
Row 6: miss 1st, dc to last 2sts, dc2tog, turn.
Rows 7 & 8: As last 2 rows.
Row 9: miss 1st, 1dc, 1B, *2dc, 1B, rep from * to last 2sts, 1dc, 1ss. Fasten off.

UNDER COLLAR

With 5.00mm hook and RS facing, work into rem loops of row 1 on upper collar.
Row 1: dc to end, 1ch, turn.
Row 2: as row 1.
Row 3: miss 1st, 1dc, *2dc in next st, 2dc, rep from * to last 2sts, 2dc in next st, 1dc, turn.
Row 4: miss 1st, dc to end, turn.
Rep row 4 twice, ending with 1ss. Fasten off.

COLLAR EDGING

With 5.00mm hook join upper and under collar sections, together
Row 1: dc to end, evenly around outer edge of both thicknesses, easing to fit, 1ch. Do not turn.
Row 2: crab st to end. Fasten off.

EDGING FOR BASE OF COAT

With 5.50mm hook and RS facing join yarn to lower right front band, crab st along lower edge. Fasten off.
Sew on buttons to correspond with buttonholes.

HAT

With 5.50mm hook, make 45ch.
Row 1: 1tr in 4th ch from hook, tr to end, 1ch, turn. [43sts]
Row 2: 2dc, *1B, 7dc, 1B**, 1dc, 4RtrB, 1dc, rep from * once, rep from * to ** once, 2dc, 3ch, turn.
Row 3: *3tr, 1CV, 3tr**, 4RtrF, rep from * once, rep from * to ** once, 1tr, 1ch.
Row 4: as row 2.
Row 5: *3tr, 1CV**, 3tr, 1twist, rep from * once, rep from * to ** once, 4tr, 1ch.
Rep last 4 rows until work measures 18cm [7in] ending with RS row. Do not turn.
Fold work in half with WS tog. Crab st the centre back seam through both thicknesses. Fasten off.

NECK EDGING

Row 1: With 5.00mm hook and RS tog, join yarn to first st, work 36dc evenly along the row, 1ch, turn.
Row 2: dc to end, 1ch, turn. Rep row 2 twice.
Do not fasten off.

HOOD EDGING

Crab st in each st along row. Fasten off.

TIES

Make 2 double twisted cords 23cm[9in] long and sew to 'corners' of hat.
Make 2 pom-poms 4cm [1½in] dia and sew to same place as ties.

[I] DINO ROAR ***

Materials: 150(200,200,200)g DK Yarn in M: 50(50,50,50)g Green: 25(50,50,50)g Lilac: Oddments of black and white: 1 black button (eye): 3 buttons (back opening): 4.50mm and 5.00mm crochet hooks.

Size: *To fit Chest:* 51-56(60-65,69-74,78-83)cm [20-22(23½-25½,27-29,30½-32½)in]
Actual chest: 59(68,77,86)cm [23¼(26¾,30¼,33¾)in]
Back length: 33(36,38,38)cm [13(14,15,15)in]
Sleeve seam: 23(26,28,31)cm [9(10,11,12)in]

Tension: 12sts and 16 rows to 9cm[3½] worked over patt on 5.00mm hook.

Abbreviations: See page 37

FRONT
With 5.00mm hook and M, make 42(48,54,60)ch.
Row 1: [RS] 1dc in 2nd ch from hook, dc ch to end, 1ch, turn [41(47,53,59)sts].
Row 2: sdc to end, 1ch, turn. First 2 rows of chart worked. Following chart for a total of 52(56,60,60) rows, ending with a WS row.
SHAPE NECK
First Side
Row 1: patt over 16(19,21,24)sts, 1ch, turn.
Row 2: sdc2tog, patt to end, 1ch, turn.
Rows 3-4: sdc to end, Fasten off.
Second Side
Row 1: miss 8(8,10,10)sts, join yarn to next st, sdc to end, 1ch, turn.
Row 2: patt to last 2sts, sdc2tog, 1ch, turn.
Rows 3-4: patt to end. Fasten off.

BACK
Work as for front, following chart for colour changes for a total of 42(46,50,50)rows.
DIVIDE FOR CENTRE BACK OPENING
First side
Row 1: With RS facing patt 20(23,26,29)sts, 1ch, turn. Work a further 13 rows on these sts. Fasten off.
Second side:
Row 1: With RS facing join to next st, dc to end, 1ch, turn. Work a further 13 rows on these sts. Fasten off.
With RS tog join shoulder seams.
BACK OPENING
With 4.50mm hook and RS facing join M to first row of left back opening, work 1dc in each row end, 1ch, turn.
Row 2: dc in each dc just worked, 1ch, turn
Rep last row once more.
NECK EDGE
Cont and work round neck:
Row 1: dc in each st and each row end around to top edge of right back opening.
Row 2: Working into row ends of right back opening, 1dc, 2ch, miss 1st 4dc, *2ch, miss 1st, 4dc, rep from * once, dc in any rem sts to end. Do not turn.
Row 3: 1ch, crab st in each st round back opening and neck edge. Fasten off.
WELTS
With 5.00mm hook and RS facing, work along rem loops of base ch, in M, make 7ch.
Row 1: dc in 2nd ch from hook, dc to end, turn.
Row 2 miss 1st, ss in back loops to end, turn. [6sts]
Row 3 ss in back loops to end [6sts], ss into next 2 base ch, turn.
Row 4 miss 2sts, ss in back loop to end, turn.
Row 5 ss in back loop to end, [6sts], ss into next base ch, turn. Last 4 rows form patt. Cont in patt to end of welt. Fasten off.

SLEEVES
With 5.00mm hook and M, make 28ch.
Row 1: [RS] 1dc in 2nd ch from hook, dc in each ch to end, 1ch, turn.
Row 2: sdc to end, 1ch, turn. [27sts]
Row 3: 2sdc in first st, sdc to last st, 2sdc in last st, 1ch, turn. Rep row 2 3 times.
Row 7: As row 3.
Row 8: As row 2. Cont working 3 rows green, 3 rows M, 3 rows lilac, 3 rows M, *at the same time* inc one st at each end of every 6th row until sleeve measures approx 19(22,24,27)cm. [7½(8½,9½,10½)in]. Fasten off.
SLEEVE SPIKES [make 8 for each sleeve]
With 4.50mm hook and lilac yarn, make 8ch.
Row 1: [RS] 1dc in 2nd ch from hook, dc in each ch to end, turn.
Row 2: miss first st, dc to end, turn. Rep last row until 1st remains. Fasten off.
Place WS tog and join spikes in pairs with 4.50mm hook, *1dc in each row end to tip of spike, 3dc in tip, dc in each row end, 1ch, join in next pair of spikes, rep from * for rem pairs. Fasten off.
Sew strip of four spikes to centre of sleeve.
CUFFS
Row 1: With 4.50mm hook and RS facing, join M to first st, 1ss, 7ch, 1dc in 2nd ch from hook, dc to end, 1ss in base of sleeve, ss in next 2sts on sleeve, turn.
Row 2: miss 2ss, ss in back loopsto end, turn. [6sts].
Row 3: 6ss in back loops, ss in next 2sts on sleeve, turn
Last 2 rows form patt. Cont in patt to sleeve end. Fasten off. Mark centre st of sleeve, place to shoulder seam with RS tog, ease sleeve to fit and join to body.

DINO DETAIL
ARM
With 4.50mm hook and green yarn, make 2ch.
Rnd 1: 8dc in 2nd ch from hook. Do not join but work in cont rnds throughout
Rnd 2: dc to end [8sts]. Rep last rnd 5 times more.
Rnd 8: 1ch, 1P, 3ch, ss in same st as 1P, *1ss 2ch 1P 3ch 1ss in next st, rep from * once. Fasten off.
Sew arm to Dino where indicated on chart.
BACK SPIKES
With 4.50mm hook and lilac yarn, make 25ch.
Row 1: 1dc in 2nd ch from hook, 1htr 1tr 1ch 1tr 1htr in next st, 2ss, 1dc 1htr 1tr 1ch 1tr 1htr 1dc in next st, *2ss, 1htr 4tr 1htr in next st, rep from * once, 2ss, (4htr in next st, ss in next 2sts)twice, 3htr in next st, ss in last st. Fasten off. Following curves of Dino, sew to the back.
EYE - FRONT
With 4.50mm hook and white yarn, make 3ch, 14htr in 3rd ch from hook, ss to join. Fasten off. Sew to position on face.
Sew small black button to centre of eye.
Embroider mouth detail with black yarn.
NOSE
With 4.50mm hook and green yarn, make 3ch, tr4tog in 3rd ch from hook. Fasten off. Sew to tip of nose.
TOES [2 for each foot].
Make as for nose. Sew to end of feet.
EYES - BACK [2 alike]
With 4.50mm hook and white yarn, make 3ch, 7tr in 3rd ch from hook, ss to join. Fasten off.
Sew to head [one slightly above the other].
Embroider eye detail with black yarn.

TO COMPLETE
Join sleeve and side seams.
Sew on buttons to correspond with buttonholes.

DINO ROAR

BACK

FRONT

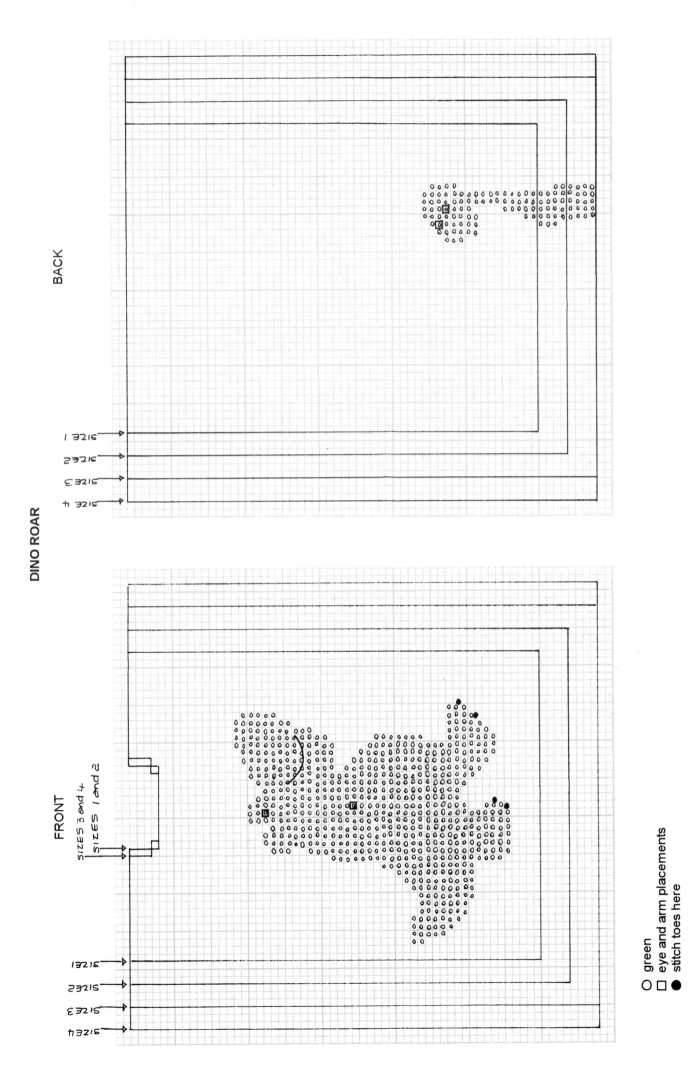

○ green
□ eye and arm placements
● stitch toes here

[J] CARLY **

Materials: *Cardigan* 275(275,350,400,450)g Chunky weight yarn (M); 75(75,100,100,100)g (C); 6.00mm & 7.00mm hooks; 5 buttons. *Beret:* 75(75,75)g (M); 25(25,25)g (C).

Size : *To fit chest:* 51(56,61,66,71)cm [20(22,24,26,28)in]
Actual Size: 58(63,68,73,78)cm [23(25,27,29,31)in]
Back length: 35(38,38,43,43)cm [13¾(15,15,17,17)in]
Sleeve seam: 23(26,29,32,35)cm [9(10¼,11½,12½13¾)in]
Beret: small, [medium, large].

Tension: 5sts and 6 rows to 5cm [2in] worked over patt on 7.00mm hook.

Abbreviations: See pg 37

CARDIGAN
BODY
With 7.00mm hook and M, make 60(65,70,75,80)ch.
Row 1: 1dc in 3rd ch from hook, dc to end, 1ch, turn.
Row 2: dc to end, 1ch, turn. Rep row 2 14(18,18,24,24)times, ending with WS row. Divide for armholes
RIGHT FRONT
Row 1: dc2tog, 12(13,14,15,16)dc, 1ch, turn [place a marker at beginning of row].
Rows 2 & 3: dc to end, 1ch, turn.
Row 4: dc to last 3sts, dc2tog, 1dc, 1ch, turn.
Rep last 3 rows 3 times.
Rep row 2 2(2,2,5,5)times. Fasten off.
BACK
Row 1: With RS facing, miss 1st, 29(32,35,38,41)dc, 1ch, turn.
Row 2: dc to end, 1ch, turn. Rep row 2 13(13,13,16,16)times. Fasten off.
LEFT FRONT
Row 1: With RS facing, miss 1st, dc to last 3sts, dc2tog, 1dc, 1ch, turn. [place marker at end of row]
Rows 2 & 3: dc to end, 1ch, turn.
Row 4: 1dc, dc2tog, dc to end, 1ch, turn.
Rep last 3 rows 3 times. Rep row 2 2(2,2,5,5)times. Fasten off. With RS tog join shoulder seams.

SLEEVES
With 7.00mm hook and M, make 29(29,29,33,33)ch.
Row 1: dc in 3rd ch from hook, dc to end, 1ch, turn.
Row 2: dc to end, 1ch, turn. Rep row 2 until sleeve measures 20(23,26,29,32)cm [8(9,10¼,11½,12½)in]. Fasten off.

CUFFS
Row 1: With 6.00mm hook and RS facing, join C to first st, 1ss, 6ch, ss in 2nd ch from hook, ss to end, 2ss to next 2sts on base of sleeve, turn.
Row 2: miss 2ss, ss in back loops to end, turn. [5sts].
Row 3: 5ss in back loops, 2ss on sleeve, turn.
Last 2 rows form patt. Cont in patt to sleeve end. Fasten off.
FRONT & NECK BAND
Row 1: With 6.00mm hook join C to lower right front, ss in each row end up right front, ss in each st to neck, ss in each row end down left front to welt, ss to end, turn.
Row 2: missing 1st at each shoulder point, ss in back loops to end, turn. On the right front for a girl and left front for a boy mark 4(4,4,4) places for button holes. [5th buttonhole will be made in welt].
Row 3: [buttonhole row]: miss 1st at shoulders *ss in back loops to first marker, 1ch, miss 1st, rep from * to end, turn.
Row 4: *ss in back loops to 1chsp, 1ss in 1chsp, rep from * to end, turn. Fasten off.
WELT
With 6.00mm hook and RS facing, work along lower edge of front band and base. Join C to first st.
Row 1: 1ss, 6ch, 1ss in 2nd ch from hook, ss to end, ss into next 2 row ends, turn.
Row 2: miss 2ss, ss in back loops, to end, turn. [5sts]
Row 3: [boys] 2ss in back loops, 1ch, miss 1st (buttonhole made), 2ss in back loops only, 2ss in base ch, [NB: (girls) ss in back loops only to end).
Row 4: miss 2sts, ss in back loops to end, turn
Row 5: ss in back loops to end, 1ss in body ch, turn.
Row 6: miss 1ss, ss in back loops to end, turn.
Row 7: ss in back loops to end, ss in body ch, turn.
Rep last 4 rows to edge of other front.
[NB (girls) make buttonhole on 2nd row from end (see row 3)]. Fasten off.
TO COMPLETE
Join sleeve seams.
Sew sleeves into armholes.
Sew on buttons to correspond with buttonholes.

BERET
Please note: for beret follow patt on page 2.

[K] EASY STRIPES *

Materials: 40(40,50,50,50)g DK yarn in 4 colours, A,B,C and D, 5.00mm & 5.50mm crochet hooks, 3 buttons.

Size : *To fit chest:* 46(51,56,61,66)cm [18(20,22,24,26)in].
Actual size: 54(59,64,69,74)cm [21(23,25,27,29)in]
Back length: 28(30,33,33,36)cm [11(12,13,13,14)in]
Sleeve seam: 18(20,22,24,26)cm [7(8,8½,9½,10¼)in]

Tension: 12sts and 16 rows to 10cm [4in] worked over patt on 5.50mm hook.

Abbreviations: See page 37

NB: Work A,B,C & D in same order throughout, regardless of the number of rows worked in each colour. This applies to all sections.

Colour rep patt
2 rows A: 2 rows B: 1 row C
2 rows D: 2 rows A: 1 row B
2 rows C: 2 rows D: 1 row A
commencing next rep with 2 rows B. Colour patt sequence applies throughout garment.

BACK
With 5.50mm hook, make 38(44,50,56,62)ch.
Row 1: [RS] 1dc in 3rd ch from hook, dc to end, 1ch, turn.
Row 2: dc to end, 1ch, turn. [36(42,48,54,60)sts]
Rep row 2, joining in colours as necessary, until back measures 28(30,33,33,36)cm [7(8,8½,9½,10¼)in] or to length required, ending with WS row. Fasten off.

FRONT

Work as back to last 3 rows. Divide for neck opening

FIRST SIDE

Row 1: patt over 14(16,19,21,24)sts, 1ch, turn.
Row 2: dc2tog, dc to end, 1ch, turn.
Row 3: dc to last 2 sts, dc2tog. Fasten off.

SECOND SIDE

Row 1: miss next 8(10,10,12,12)sts, join yarn to next st, 1ch, dc to end, 1ch, turn.
Row 2: dc to last 2sts, dc2tog, 1ch, turn.
Row 3: dc2tog, dc to end, do not fasten off.

SHOULDER OPENING

Row 1: 1ch, dc to end, 1ch, turn.
Row 2: [buttonhole row], 1dc, 1ch, miss 1st *4(4,4,5, 5)dc,1ch,miss 1st, rep from *once, dc to end,1ch, turn
Join right shoulder seam with RS tog. Do not fasten off.

NECK EDGE

Row 3: 1dc in each st, each chsp, and each row end around neck and shoulder edges. Do not turn, 1ch.
Row 4: crab st all round. Fasten off.

SLEEVES

With 5.50mm hook, make 20(20,20,24,26)ch.
Row 1: 1dc in 3rd ch from hook, dc to end, 1ch, turn

Row 2: dc to end, 1ch, turn.
Row 3: 2dc in 1st st, dc to last st, 2dc in last st, 1ch, turn.
Cont to inc one st at each end of every 3rd row, until sleeve measures 18(20,22,24,26)cm [7(8,8½,9½, 10¼)in] or to length required. Fasten off.
Mark centre st on last row.

SLEEVE EDGING

With 5.50mm hook and RS facing, join yarn to any st at base of sleeve. Crab st to end, join with ss. Fasten off.

LOWER EDGING

Row 1: With 5.50mm hook and RS facing join yarn to any st at lower edge, 1ch, dc to end, ss to join.
Do not turn, 1ch.
Row 2: crab st to end, ss to join. Fasten off.

TO COMPLETE

Overlap buttonhole band at shoulder edge over first few stitches of back and sew in place.
Join sleeves to body with RS tog matching marked stitch of sleeve to shoulder seam, sew sleeves to body easing to fit.
Sew on buttons to correspond with buttonholes.
Make 4 x 4cm[1½in] pompoms and stitch to front of sweater as shown.

[L] TWEED SUIT ***

Materials: *Jacket:* 125(125 125,150,175)g Yarn A: 100(100, 100,125,150)g Yarn B. *Skirt:* 75(75,75,100,100)g Yarn A: 50(50,50,75,75)g Yarn B: 3.50, and 4.00mm hooks: 7(8) buttons, 2cm [¾in] wide elastic (to fit waist),

Size:
To fit chest: 56(61,66,71,76)cm [22(24,26,28,30)in]
Actual size of jacket: 64(69,74,79,84)cm [25(27,29,31,33)in]
Back length: 29(31,33,35,37)cm [11½(12¼,13,13¾,14½)in]
Sleeve seam: 20(22,24,26,28)cm 8(8¾,9½,10¼,11)in] or length required. *Skirt length:*23(23,25,28,31)cm [9(9,10,11,12¼)in]
Skirt waist up to: 51(51,56,56,61)cm[20(20,22,22,24)in] (or djustable)

Tension: 8sts and 10 rows to 5cm [2in] worked over patt on 4.00mm hook.

Abbreviations: See page 37

JACKET
BODY

Worked in one piece to armholes.   With 4.00mm hook and A, make 98(106,114,122,130)ch.
Row 1: [RS]1dc in 3rd ch from hook, dc to end, 1ch, turn.
Row 2: dc to end, join in B, 1ch, turn.
Row 3: 2dc,*miss 1st, 1dc 2 rows below, 1dc, rep from * to last st, 1dc, 1ch, turn.
Row 4: as row 2, joining in A.
Row 5: 1dc, *miss 1st, 1dc 2 rows below, 1dc, rep from * to end, 1ch, turn.
Row 6: As row 2. Join in B. Rows 3-6 incl form patt.
Cont in patt until work measures 15(18,20,22,24)cm, [6(7,8,8¾,9½)in] or length required, ending on a WS row.   Divide for armholes

RIGHT FRONT

Row 1: 23(25,27,29,31)dc, 1ch, turn.

Work 19 rows in patt.

Shape Neck

Row 1: ss over 6sts, 1ss 1dc in next st, patt to end, 1ch, turn.
Row 2: patt to last 2sts, dc2tog, 1ch, turn.
Row 3: patt to end, 1ch, turn. Work 2 rows in patt.
Row 6: as row 2.
Rows 7 & 8: patt to end. Fasten off.

BACK

Row 1: With RS facing join in yarn, miss next st, 49(53,57,61,65)dc, 1ch, turn. Work 27 rows in patt on these sts. Fasten off.

LEFT FRONT

With RS facing join in yarn, miss next st.
Row 1: patt to end, 1ch, turn [23(25,27,29,31)sts].
Work 19 more rows in patt.

Shape Neck

Row 1: patt to last 6sts, 1ch, turn.
Row 2: dc2tog, patt to end, 1ch, turn.
Row 3: patt to end, 1ch, turn. Work 2 rows in patt.
Row 6: dc2tog, patt to end, 1ch, turn.
Rows 7 & 8: patt to end. Fasten off.
With RS tog, join shoulder seams on WS.

EDGING

Row 1: With 3.50mm hook join yarn A to first st at base of front.
Work 1dc in each row end up right front, round neck and down left front,miss 1st at each shoulder seam, turn
Row 2: ss in each st to shoulder seam, miss 1st, ss to top edge of right front edge, 1ss, (3ch, miss 1st, 9ss) 4(4,5,5,5)times, 3ch, miss 1st, ss to end, 1ch, turn. [5(5,6,6,6) buttonholes made].
Row 3: crab st around garment, ss to join. Fasten off.

SLEEVES

With 4.00mm hook and A, make 30ch.
Row 1: 1dc in 3rd ch from hook, dc to end, 1ch, turn.
Follow and keep patt as for body, inc 1st at each end of every 6th row until sleeve measures 17(17,20,20, 20)cm [7(7,8,8,8)in]. Cont in patt without inc until sleeve measures 20(22,24,26,28)cm [8(8¾,9½,10¼, 11)in] or to length required. Fasten off.
With RS tog join sleeve seams on WS. Sew sleeves into jacket.

SLEEVE EDGE

With 4.00mm hook and A, crab st round edge of sleeve.

POCKETS

FLAPS

With 4.00mm hook and B, make 18ch.
Row 1: 1dc in 3rd ch from hook, dc to end, 1ch, turn.
Row 2: dc to end, 1ch, turn. Work in patt for 6 rows.
Row 9: ss to end. *Do not turn.* Change to 3.50mm hook.

EDGE

Row 1: dc in each st and each row end round 3 rem edges of flap, working 3dc into corners. *Do not turn.*
Row 2: 1ch, crab st round 3 sides. Fasten off.

Sew pocket flaps to front of jacket [see illustration].
Sew buttons to correspond with buttonholes.
Sew a button to centre of each pocket flap.

SKIRT

With 4.00mm hook and A, make 92(92,100,100, 108)ch.
Row 1: 1dc in 2nd ch from hook, dc to end, 1ch, turn.
Follow patt as for body until work measures approx 20(20,22,25,28)cm [8(8,9,10,11)in] or length required, ending with a WS facing row.

WAISTBAND

Row 1: With 3.50mm hook and A, dc to end, 1ch, turn.
Row 2: dc to end, 1ch, turn. Rep last row 6 times. Fasten off.
Fold skirt in half and with WS tog, sew centre back seam. Fold waistband down and catch-stitch in place, leaving a small opening. Thread elastic through the channel made. Close the opening.

EDGING

Wtih 4.00mm hook and A, working along the starting ch, crab st to end, ss to join. Fasten off.

[M] MAGICAL TRICKS ****

Materials: 250(275:300:325)g in total of DK yarn - the more colours used, better the effect, 3 small black buttons (eyes for moon and bunny), 4 small black beads (dove eyes),6 buttons, sequin stars (optional), metallic thread for attaching sequins (optional), 4.50mm and 5.00mm hooks.
Size: *To fit chest:* 51-56(56-61-61-66:66-71)cm [20-22(22-24:24-26:26-28)in
Actual size: 62(68,74,80)cm [24½(26¾,29,31½)in]
Back length: 34(34,38,38)cm [13½(13½,15,15)in]
Sleeve seam: 19(19,23,23)cm [7½(7½,9,9)in]

Tension: 8sts and 10 rows to 6cm[2½in]worked over patt on 5.00mm hook
Abbreviations. see pg 37

BACK

With 5.00mm hook, make 46(50,54,58)ch.
Row 1: [RS and first row of the chart] 1dc in 3rd ch from hook, dc to end, 1ch, turn.
Row 2: 2dc, 1B, *3dc, 1B, rep from * to last 2sts, 2dc, 1ch, turn.
Row 3: dc to end, 1ch, turn. Rep last row, following chart for colour changes. Fasten off.

MAGICAL TRICKS

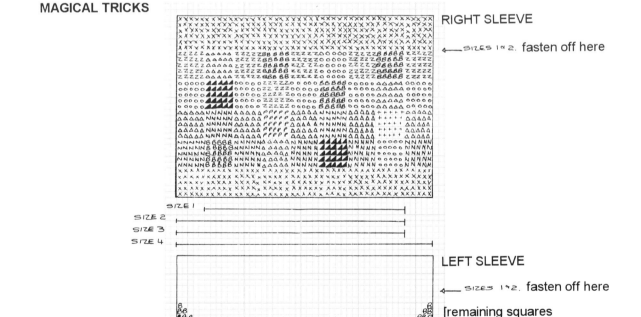

RIGHT SLEEVE

← SIZES 1 & 2. fasten off here

SIZE 1
SIZE 2
SIZE 3
SIZE 4

LEFT SLEEVE

← SIZES 1 & 2. fasten off here

[remaining squares worked in purple]

MAGICAL TRICKS

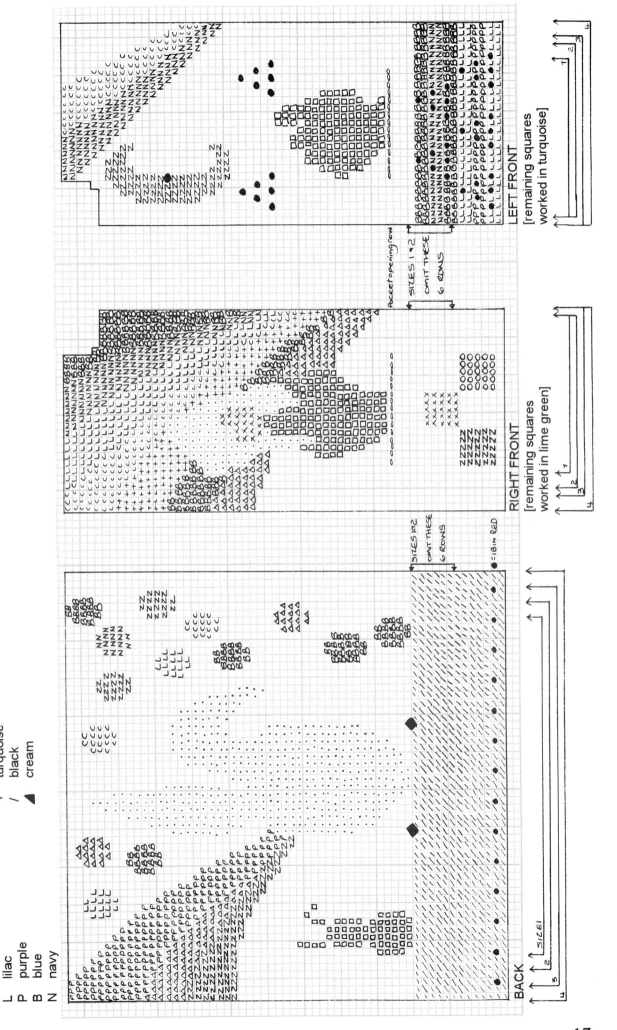

Key:

- ◆ stitch paws here
- ● 1 bobble
- ○ chsp for pocket opening
- △ green
- z yellow
- L lilac
- P purple
- B blue
- N navy
- □ pink
- C cerise
- O orange
- x red
- • white
- + turquoise
- / black
- ◤ cream

LEFT FRONT [remaining squares worked in turquoise]

RIGHT FRONT [remaining squares worked in lime green]

BACK

SIZES 1 & 2 OMIT THESE 6 ROWS

POCKET OPENING ROW

= 18 IN RED

17

FRONTS

NB: Both fronts are alike except for the neck shaping.
With 5.00mm hook, make 22(24,26,28)ch.
Row 1: [RS and first row of chart] 1dc in 3rd ch from hook, 1dc in each ch to end, 1ch, turn.
Working in dc, follow chart to pocket opening row.
Pocket opening row: With WS facing patt over 5(5, 6,6)sts, 15ch, miss 15sts, dc to end, 1ch, turn.
Working in dc, follow charts for colour changes and neck shaping. Fasten off.

POCKET LINING

With 5.00mm hook, join yarn to pocket opening, 1ch, 1dc in same place, 13dc, 2dc in last st, 1ch, turn.
Row 2: dc to end, 1ch, turn. Rep last row 11 times.
Fasten off. Sew 3 sides of pocket lining to inside of jacket. With RS tog, join shoulder seams.

BUTTONHOLE BAND

With 4.50mm hook and RS facing join yarn to front edge. Work into each row end along centre front.
Row 1: 1ss in each row end, turn.
Row 2: 1ss in back loops only to end, turn.
Rep last row 3 times. Mark position of 5 buttons.
Row 6: [buttonhole row] *ss in back loop only to marker, 1ch, miss 1st, rep from * to end.
Rep row 2 3 times. Fasten off.

BUTTON BAND

Rep 1st row of buttonhole band once.
Rep 2nd row of buttonhole band 8 times. Fasten off.

WELT

With 4.50mm hook and RS facing join yarn to base of jacket, make 7ch.
Row 1: 1dc in 3rd ch from hook, dc to end, 1ss into body, turn.
Row 2: miss 1ss, ss in back loops to end, turn. [6sts]
Row 3: [work buttonhole here or 3 rows from end of welt] 3ss in back loop only, 1ch, miss 1st, 2ss in back loop, 1ss into base ch. Alternatively work Row 5.
Row 4: As row 2.
Row 5: 6ss in back loops, 1ss into base ch, turn.
Rep last 2 rows to end. Fasten off.
Sew on buttons to correspond with buttonholes.

SLEEVES

With 5.00mm hook, make 36(41,41,46)ch.
Row 1: [RS and first row of chart] 1dc in 3rd ch from hook, 1dc in each ch to end, 1ch, turn.
Working in dc, follow charts to end.

CUFFS

With 4.50mm hook and RS facing, join yarn to first st, make 7ch.
Row 1: 1dc in 3rd ch from hook, dc to end, ss into next 2sts of sleeve, turn.
Row 2: miss 2ss, ss in back loops to end, turn [6sts]
Row 3: 6ss in back loops only, 2ss into sleeve, turn.
Rep last 2 rows to end of sleeve. Fasten off.
Mark centre st on last row of sleeve and place to shoulder seam with RS tog, join sleeves to body.
Join side and sleeve seams.

HOOD

With 5.00mm hook, make 64(68,72,72)ch.
Row 1: [RS] 1dc in 3rd ch from hook, 1dc in each ch to end, 1ch, turn.
Row 2: 1dc, 1B, *3dc, 1B, rep from * to last st, 1dc, 1ch, turn.
Row 3: dc to end, join in next colour, 1ch, turn.
Rows 4 & 5: dc to end, 1ch, turn.
Row 6: Rep row 3. Rows 4-6 incl form patt.
Cont in patt until work measures approx 18(18,20, 20)cm [7(7,8,8)in]. Do not fasten off.
Fold hood in half with WS tog and crab stitch to close centre back seam. With RS tog, join neck edges of hood and body omitting front bands.

DETAILS OF DESIGN

MAGIC WAND

With 4.50mm hook and black, make 19ch, 1ss in 3rd ch from hook, ss to end. Fasten off.
With white yarn, embroider tip of wand. Sew wand in

position [see illustration].
FINGER: With 4.50mm hook and pink, make 5ch.
Row 1: 1dc in 3rd ch from hook, dc to end, 1ch, turn.
Row 2: dc to end, 2ch, turn.
Row 3: 1dc in 2nd ch from hook, dc to end, 1ch, turn.
Rows 4-8: As row 2 turning with 1ch.
Fasten off leaving a tail of yarn.
Sew fingers in position, shaping at the same time.

MOON FEATURES

Attach small black button for eye. Embroider mouth.
BUNTING: With 4.50mm hook *5ch, 1dc in 2nd ch from hook, 1htr, 1tr, 1dtr, join in next col yarn, rep from * 6 times. Fasten off.
Using photograph as a guide, attach bunting to body.
THUMB: With 4.50mm hook and pink yarn, make 5ch
Row 1: 1dc in 3rd ch from hook, dc to end, 1ch, turn
Row 2: dc to end, 1ch, turn.
Row 3: 1dc, 2dc in next st, dc to end, 1ch, turn.
Rep row 2 twice.
Row 6: 2dc, 2dc in next st, dc to end, 1ch, turn.
Row 7: as row 2.
Row 8: 2dc in first st, dc to last st, 2dc in last st, 1ch, turn. Rep row 2 twice.
Row 11: 5dc, 1ss, turn.
Row 12: miss 1ss, 1ss in next st, dc to end, 1ch, turn.
Row 13: 4dc, 1ss. Fasten off.
Sew thumb to hand. Embroider fingers.
CARD DETAILS: With red yarn, embroider 'A' on card. Sew a sequin to centre of card (optional).
Embroider initials or 'ABC' on blocks.
BUNNY PAWS [2 alike]
With 5.00mm hook and white, make slip knot which slides from tail end, 2ch [NB see pg 000].
Rnd 1: 8dc in 2nd ch from hook. [Mark end of rnd]. Do not join. Work in cont rnds unless otherwise stated.
Rnd 2: *1dc, 2dc in next st, rep from *to end [12sts]
Rnd 3: dc to end [12]. Rep rnd 3 3 times. 1ss.
[NB: WS of fabric is RS of work].
Rnd 7: Pinch ends of last rnd tog. Work through both thicknesses, 5dc, 1ss to close. Fasten off.
Using photograph as a guide, sew paws into position.
CHEEKS: Make 2 pom-poms 3cm dia. Sew centrally to lower half of face.
NOSE: 3.50mm hook and black yarn, make 3ch, 5trpuff in 3rd ch from hook. Fasten off. Sew nose to face bet and above cheeks. Attach 2 buttons for eyes
SMALL BUNNY TAIL
With 4.50mm hook and white yarn, make 3ch, tr5tog in 3rd ch from hook. Fasten off. Sew tail to bunny.
DOVE [2 alike]
Head and body: With 4.50mm hook, make 2ch.
Rnd 1: 8dc in 2nd ch from hook. Do not join but work in cont rnds unless otherwise stated.
[NB: The WS of the fabric is RS of work].
Rnd 2 & 3: dc to end.
Rnd 4: (dc2tog)4 times.
Rnd 5: 2dc in each st to end.
Rnd 6: *1dc, 2dc in next st, rep from *to end [12sts]
Rnd 7: dc to end.
Rnd 8: *2dc, 2dc in next st, rep from *to end [16sts]
Rnd 9: as rnd 7
Rnd 10: dc2tog to end [8sts].
Rnd 11: dc2tog to end [4sts], 1ss. Fasten off.
Wings[2 alike]: With 4.50mm hook, make 3ch, 1dc in 2nd ch from hook, (1dc, 1htr, 3tr, 1htr, 1dc) in next st. Cont working round wing using rem loop of starting ch, 1dc, 1ss. Fasten off. Sew wings to sides of body.
Tail: Wind a piece of yarn 4 times around 3 fingers. Fold loops in half and tie together in a figure of 8.
Sew tail to lower back of dove.
Beak: With 4.50mm hook and orange yarn, make 2ch, 1dc in 2nd ch from hook. Fasten off.
Sew on beak and attach beads for eyes to doves.
Sew pom-pom to sleeve.
Sew sequin stars to body (optional).

[N] CUTE LITTLE ***
BABY FACE

Materials: 150(200,200,250,250)g DK yarn in M: 50(50,50,50,50)g in peach for face, oddments in white for bonnet: yellow for hair, green for dummy, 4.50mm and 5.00mm crochet hooks, 2 black buttons with shanks for eyes: 2 buttons for shoulder opening.

Size: *To fit chest:* 51(56,61,66,71)cm[20(22,24,26,28,)in]
Actual size: 58(63,68,73,78)cm [23(25,27,29,31)in]
Back length: 34(39,39,42,42)cm [13½(15½,15½,16½,16½)in]
Sleeve seam: 19(23,25,28,28)cm [7½(9,10,11,11)in]

Tension: 12sts and 16 rows to 9cm [3½in] worked on 5.00mm hook over patt.

Abbreviations: See page 37

FRONT

With 5.00mm hook make 45(49,53,57,61)ch.
Row 1: [RS] 1dc in 2nd ch from hook, dc to end, 1ch, turn. [First row of chart worked].
Row 2: 1ch, sdc to end, 1ch, turn.
Follow chart for colour changes and work in sdc for a total of 55(61,61,65,65) rows.

SHAPE NECK
First Side
Row 1: [WS] 17(18,20,22,24)sdc, 1ch, turn.
Row 2: sdc2tog, sdc to end, 1ch, turn.
Rows 3-4 incl: sdc to end, 1ch, turn. Fasten off.
Second Side
Row 1: With WS facing miss next 8(10,10,10,10)sts, sdc to end, 1ch, turn.
Row 2: sdc to last 3sts, sdc2tog, 1sdc, 1ch, turn.
Rows 3-4 incl: sdc to end, 1ch, turn. Fasten off.

BACK

Make as for front omitting colour changes, work 59(65, 65,69,69) rows in sdc. Fasten off.

NECK & SHOULDER
With RS tog join right shoulder seam.
Row 1: With 4.50mm hook and RS facing join yarn to left front shoulder, dc along shoulder seam, 1ch, turn
Row 2: dc to end, 1ch, turn.
Row 3: [buttonhole row], 6dc, miss 1st, 2ch, 1dc, dc to last 3sts, miss 1st, 2ch, 1dc. Do not turn but cont round neck and shoulder, placing 1st in each st and row end. Do not turn, 1ch.
Row 4: crab st to end. Fasten off.

SLEEVES

With 5.00mm hook, make 43ch.
Row 1: 1dc in 2nd ch from hook, dc to end, 1ch, turn
Row 2: sdc to end, 1ch, turn.
Rep row 2 until work measures 18(20,23,25,25)cm [7(8,9,10,10)in] or length required. Fasten off.

CUFFS
With RS facing and 5.00mm hook join yarn to base of sleeve.
Row 1: 7ch, 1ss in 3rd ch from hook, ss to end, 2ss to base of sleeve, turn [6sts].
Row 2: miss last 2ss made, ss in back loops to end, turn.

Row 3: 6ss in back loops, ss into next 2sts of sleeve, turn
Rep last 2 rows to other edge of sleeve. Fasten off.

FACE FEATURES

NOSE: [NB: WS of fabric is RS of work.]
With 5.00mm hook and peach yarn, make 2ch.
Rnd 1: 8dc in 2nd ch from hook, ss to join, 1ch.
Rnd 2: 2dc in each st to end, ss to join. Fasten off leaving 25cm [10in] of yarn.
Sew to centre of face, padding with a little matching yarn before closing opening.
EYES: Attach black buttons to face just above nose, approx 2cm[¾in] apart.
DUMMY: With 5.00mm hook and green yarn work first 2 rnds as nose.
Rnd 3: 1ch, *1dc, 2dc in next st, rep from * to end, ss to join. Fasten off.
DUMMY RING: Make a 5cm [2in] double twisted cord with matching yarn. Thread both ends through centre of ring on dummy, knot in place and sew to face under nose [See illustration].
BONNET FRILL: With 5.00mm hook and white yarn make 82ch.
Row 1: 1dc in 3rd ch from hook, dc to end, 1ch, turn. [81sts]
Row 2: 1dc, miss 1st, *5tr in next st, miss 1st, 1dc, miss 1st, rep from * to last st, 1dc, 1ss in last st. Fasten off. Sew frill round head, placing ends of frill level with row 6(11,11,11,11) on face.
BONNET TIES: [2 alike]
Cut 2 lengths of yarn 90cm [32in], fold each length in half and make twisted cord.
Attach each end of cord to ends of bonnet frill with a few stitches. Tie in a knot or bow under chin.
HAIR: Wind yellow yarn around 4 fingers 5 times. Tie a length of yarn round centre of bundle and sew to head just below frill.
WELTS [alike]
With RS facing and 5.00mm hook join yarn to base of sweater.
Row 1: 7ch, ss in 2nd ch from hook, ss to end, ss in base of sleeve, turn.
Row 2: miss first ss, ss in back loop only to end, turn.
Row 3: 6ss in back loops only, ss into next 2 starting ch, turn.
Row 4: miss first 2sts, ss in back loop only to end, turn.
Row 5: 6ss in back loops only, ss into next starting ch, turn. Last 4 rows form patt. Repeat for length required. Fasten off.

TO COMPLETE

Mark centre st on last row of sleeve. With RS tog, match with shoulder seam, and sew sleeve to body, easing to fit.
Join underarm and side seams in one.
Sew buttons to shoulder to correspond with buttonholes.

BABY FACE

☐ peach

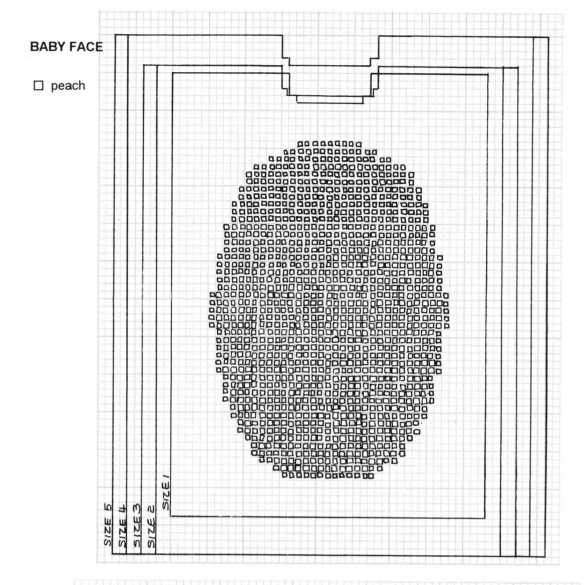

SIZE 5   SIZE 4   SIZE 3   SIZE 2   SIZE 1

BOW TIE

– white
[remainder in
blue]

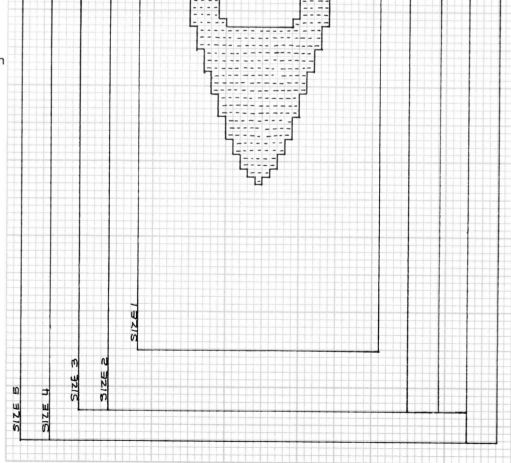

SIZE 5   SIZE 4   SIZE 3   SIZE 2   SIZE 1

[O] BOW TIE ***

Materials: 175(200,200,250,250)g in DK yarn in M, 30(50,50,50,50)g in C, oddment of DK for bow tie, 4.50mm and 5.00mm crochet hooks,6(6,6,6,6) buttons [front detail & back opening], 2 contrasting buttons[(cuffs),

Size: *Size to fit chest:* 46-51 (55,61-66,71,76)cm [18-20(22,24-26.28,30)in]

Actual Size: 54(61,68,75,82)cm[21¼(24,26¾,29½,32¼)in]

Back length: 29(34,34,38,38)cm [11½ (13½,13½,15,15)in]

Sleeve seam: 18(21,23,26,28)cm [7(8,9,10,11)in]

Tension: 12sts and 16 rows to 9cm [3½in]worked on 5.00mm hook over pattern.

Abbreviations: See page37

FRONT

In M and 5.00mm hook, make 35(43,51,59,67)ch.

Row 1: [RS] dc in 2nd ch from hook and each ch to end, 1ch, turn. [First row of chart worked].

Row 2: sdc to end, 1ch, turn. Work rem rows of chart, following colour changes. Fasten off.

BACK

Work as front for 32(40,40,44,44)rows. Divide for back opening.

Next row [RS is now facing] 16(20,24,28,32)sdc, 1ch, turn. Rep this row 14 times. Fasten off.

With RS facing, join yarn to next st, sdc to end, 1ch, turn. 16(20,24,28,32)sts. Rep last row 14 times. Fasten off.

BACK OPENING EDGE

With 4.50mm hook, rejoin yarn to right back opening, 1dc in each row end round. Fasten off.

COLLAR

FIRST SIDE

With 5.00mm hook and M, make 27ch.

Row 1: 1dc in 3rd ch from hook, dc to end, 1ch, turn. [26sts].

Row 2: 22dc, ss in next st, turn.

Row 3: miss first st, ss in next st, ss 1ch 1dc in next st, dc to end, 1ch, turn.

Row 4: 1ch, 19dc, ss, turn.

Row 5: miss first st, 1ss, 1ss 1ch 1dc in next st, 5dc, 1ch, turn.

Row 6: 4dc, 1ss, turn.

Row 7: miss first st, 1ss, 1ss 1ch 1dc in next st, 2dc, 1ch. Do not turn. Work 1dc in next 3 row ends, ss in next unworked dc on row 5, 1ch.

Row 8: dc to end, 1ch, turn.

Row 9: 12dc, 1ch, turn.

Row 10: dc to end, turn.

Row 11: ss in each st and each row end round outer edges, omitting starting ch. Fasten off.

SECOND SIDE

Work as for side 1, for first 10 rows. Fasten off. Do not turn work. Join yarn to first st of last row, ss all round. Fasten off.

Join collar by sewing base of collar to centre 'V' on front. Catch stitch top edges of collar to shoulder seam. Join front and back shoulder seams.

NECK EDGING

With 4.50mm hook and RS facing, join M to top right back opening with 1dc, 2ch, miss next st, 8dc, 2ch, miss 1st, dc to end. Fasten off. [2 buttonholes made].

With RS facing, join yarn to other side of back opening and dc round front neck. Fasten off.

Crab st round back opening and neck edge. Fasten off.

WELTS

Row 1: With 4.50mm hook and M, join to lower edge, 1ch, dc to end, 2ch, turn. 33(41,49,57,65)sts.

Row 2: 1RtrB, *1RtrF, 1RtrB, rep from * to last st, 1htr, 2ch, turn.

Row 3: 1RtrB, *1RtrF, 1RtrB, rep from * to last st, 1htr, 2ch, turn.

Row 4: as row 2. Fasten off.

SLEEVES

With 5.00mm hook and M, make 25ch.

Row 1: 1dc in 3rd ch from hook, dc to end, 1ch, turn. [23]sts.

Row 2: sdc to end, 1ch, turn.

Row 3: As row 2.

Row 4: 2sdc in first st, sdc to last st, 2sdc in last st, 1ch, turn. Repeat row 2 4 times.

Rep rows 4-8 until sleeve measures 15(18,20,23, 25)cm [6(7,8,9,10)in]or length required. Fasten off. Mark centre st on last row.

CUFFS

Row 1: with 4.50mm hook and RS facing, join C to base of sleeve, 1ch, dc to end. Fasten off, do not turn.

Row 2: with RS facing, join C to first st, 3ch, tr to end, 2ch, turn.

Row 3: 1RtrB, *1RtrF, 1RtrB, rep from * to last st, 1htr. Fasten off.

Join sleeve to body by matching marked st with shoulder seam. Crab st sleeves to body on RS easing to fit.

BOW TIE

With 5.00mm hook and oddment of yarn, make 28ch, ss to join.

Rnd 1: 1ch, dc to end, ss to join. 1ch, do not turn.

Rnd 2: dc to end,ss to join,1ch,do not turn.

Rnd 3: crab st to end, ss to join. Fasten off.

Join yarn to ch and with RS facing crab st to end, ss to join. Fasten off.

Fold in half with seam in centre. Gather centre with matching yarn. Sew to centre front neck.

TO COMPLETE

With RS tog join side and underarm seams.

Stitch 4 buttons to centre front, 2 to back opening and 1 to each cuff.

[P] BASKETWEAVE WAISTCOAT ***

Materials: 150(200,200)g DK yarn, 4.50mm and 5.00mm crochet hooks, 3 buttons.
Size: *To fit chest:* 51(61,71)cm [20(24,28)in]
Actual size: 56(66,76)cm [22(26,30)in]
Back length: 28(30.5,35.5)cm [11(12,14)in]
Tension: 9sts and 5rows to 5cm[2in] in patt on 5.00mm hook
Abbreviations: See page 37
Notes for keeping stitch patt continuous
1. Commence each row with 2ch. 2. End each row with 1htr.
3. A in chart = work RtrB in each st on WS row and RtrF in each st on RS row. 4. B in chart = work RtrF in each st on WS row and RtrB in each st on RS row. 5. To dec at **beg** of row 2ch, Rtr2tog. To dec at **end** of row work to last 3sts, Rtr2tog, 1htr. 6. Always place a marker at first dec point.

BODY

With 5.00mm hook make 102(118,134)ch.
Row 1: 1tr in 4th ch from hook, 1tr in each ch to end, 2ch, turn. Follow the chart overleaf for the size needed.
RIGHT FRONT
Work on first 20(24,28)sts following chart.
BACK
Miss 8sts, rejoin yarn to next st and follow correct size chart for back shaping.

LEFT FRONT
Miss 8sts rejoin yarn to next st and follow correct size chart for left front.
LEFT FRONT BAND
With RS facing and 4.50mm hook join to marked st on left front, dc down front checking you have the right number of sts to make the band lie flat, 1ch, turn.
Row 2: dc to end, turn.
Row 3: *[NB: for boys work row 3 of Right Front Band]* dc to last st, ss in last st. Fasten off.
Mark 3 buttons evenly spaced on the band.
RIGHT FRONT BAND
With RS facing and 4.50mm hook, join yarn to base of Right Front, 1ch, dc to marker with the same number of stitches as on the left front, turn.
Row 2: dc to end, 1ch, turn.
Row 3: [buttonhole row] *dc to marker, 2ch, miss 2sts, rep from * to end, continue in dc up right shoulder, round back neck, and down left front to marker. Fasten off neatly.
ARMHOLE EDGE
With RS facing and 4.50mm hook, join yarn to underarm. Work dc evenly round armhole, ss to join. *Do not turn.*
Row 2: Crab st to end, ss to join. Fasten off. Check both armholes have an equal number of sts.
Sew on the 3 buttons.

[Q] SAIL AWAY ***
[Waistcoat and Cardigan]

Materials: *Waistcoat:* 125(150,150)g DK yarn
Cardigan: 175(200,200)g DK yarn
4.50mm and 5.00mm crochet hooks: 6(7,7) buttons: oddment DK yarn for edging.
Size: *To fit chest:* 51(56,61)cm [20(22,24)in]
Actual size: 62(67,72)cm [24½(26½,28½)in]
Back length: 29(31,33)cm [11½(12¼,13)in]
Sleeve seam: 17(21,25)cm [6½(8¼,10)in]
Tension: 14sts and 18 rows to 10cm[4in] worked on 5.00mm hook.
Abbreviations: See page 37

WAISTCOAT
BODY

With 5.00mm hook, make 89(96,103)ch.
Row 1: [RS]dc in 3rd ch from hook, dc to end, 1ch, turn.
Row 2: dc to end, 1ch, turn. [88(95,102)sts].
Rep last row until work measures approx 15(17,19)cm [6(6¾,7½)in] or length required, ending on WS row.
RIGHT FRONT
Row 1: 19(21,23)dc, 1ch, turn.
Row 2: dc2tog, dc to end, 1ch, turn.
Row 3: 2dc in 1st st, dc to end, 1ch, turn [place marker at front edge of this row]. Rep last 2 rows once.
Row 6: dc to last st, 1htr, 1ch, turn.

Row 7: 2dc in 1st st, dc to end, 1ch, turn.
Row 8: dc to end, 1ch, turn. Rep last 2 rows once.
Row 11-12: dc to end, 1ch, turn.
Row 13: As Row 7.
Rows 14 & 15: As row 8.
Row 16: dc to last st, 1htr, 1ch, turn.
Row 17: 2dc in 1st st, dc to end, 1ch, turn.
Row 18: dc to end, 1ch, turn.
Rep last 2 rows once and row 17 once more.
Row 22: dc to last st, 1htr. Fasten off.
BACK
Row 1: With RS facing and 5.00mm hook miss 4sts, join yarn in next st, 1ch, 42(45,48)dc, 1ch, turn.
Row 2: dc2tog, dc to last 2sts, dc2tog, 1ch, turn.
Row 3: dc to end, 1ch, turn. Rep last 2 rows once.
Row 6: dc to end, 1ch, turn.
Rep last row 16 times. Fasten off.
LEFT FRONT
Row 1: With RS facing and 5.00mm hook miss 4sts, join yarn in next st, 1ch, dc to end, 1ch, turn [19(21, 23)sts]. Follow patt as right front, reversing all shapings. Join shoulder seams with RS together commencing at armhole edge, 12(14,16)sts for shoulder leaving rem sts for collar. Turn to RS and fold collar lapels back.
ARMHOLE EDGE
With 4.50mm hook join M yarn to underarm, 1ch. 1dc in each st and row end all round, ss to join. Fasten off.

BASKETWEAVE

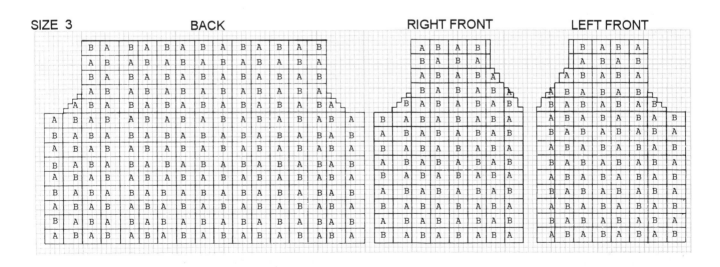

BORDER EDGE

With 4.50mm hook and WS facing join yarn to start of left front.

Row 1: 1ch, dc up left front, round collar and down right front, placing 1dc in each dc, 1dc in each row end and 3dc in corners of collar, 1ch, turn.
Evenly mark for 6(7,7) buttons.

Row 2: (buttonhole row) *dc to button marker, miss 1ch, 1ch, rep from * to end placing 3dc in corners, 1ch, turn.

Row 3: dc to end, work 3dc in corners. Fasten off.
Attach buttons to correspond with buttonholes.

COLLAR

With 5.00mm hook and inside of garment facing join yarn to first st on right lapel.

Row 1: Work dc along right lapel, back neck and left lapel, 1ch, turn.

Row 2: dc to end, 1ch, turn.
Rep last row until collar measures approx 9(10,10)cm [3½(4,4)in]. Fasten off.

COLLAR EDGING

With 4.50mm hook, C yarn, and RS of collar together, work between the marked sts, commencing at right front, crab stitch all round. Fasten off.

CARDIGAN

Make up exactly as for waistcoat, omitting armhole edging.4

SLEEVES

With 5.00mm hook, make 23(25,27)ch.

Row 1: [RS] 1dc in 3rd ch from hook, dc to end, 1ch, turn

Row 2: dc to end, 1ch, turn.

Row 3: 2dc in first st, dc to last st, 2dc in last st, 1ch, turn. Rep row 2 3 times.
The last 4 rows form patt. Cont in patt until work measures 17(21,25)cm [6 (8¼,10)in] or length required. Fasten off.
Join sleeve seams on WS. Turn sleeves RS outside and with RS together, sew sleeves into armholes.

[R] LOVELY BUBBLY ***

Materials: 300(350:400:450:500)g DK yarn in a mixture of colours: 6(6,7,7,7) buttons: 4.50mm,5.00mm and 5.50mm crochet hooks.

Size: *To fit chest*: 56(61,66,71,76)cm [22(24,26,28,30)in]
Actual size: 60(66,72,78,84)cm [23½(26,28½,30½,33)in]
Back length: 38(38,45,45,45)cm [15(15,17¾,17¾,17¾)in]
Sleeve seam: 15(18,21,24,27)cm [6(7,8¼,9½,10½)in]

Tension: 9rows and 8sts to 6cm[2½in] worked over patt on 5.00mm hook.

Abbreviations: See page 37

BODY

With 5.00mm hook, make 84(92,100,108,116)ch.

Row 1: [RS], 1dc in 3rd ch from hook, dc to end, 1ch, turn.

Row 2: 1dc,1B,*3dc,1B,rep from * to last st, 1dc, 1ch, turn. [83(91,99,107,115)st]

Row 3: dc to end, 1ch, turn.

Row 4: 3dc *1B, 3dc, rep from * to end, 1ch, turn.

Row 5: dc to end, 1ch, turn. Rows 2-5 incl form patt.
Cont in patt until work measures 13(13,15,15,15)cm [5(5,6,6,6)in], ending with a WS row.

Next row: [pocket opening]: 2(3,4,5,6)dc, 15ch, miss 15sts, dc to last 17(18,19,20,21)sts,15ch,miss 15sts, dc to end,1ch, turn.
Cont in patt until work measures 20(20,25,25,25)cm [8(8,10,10,10)in] ending with a WS row or length required. Divide for armholes.

RIGHT FRONT

Patt over 19(21,23,25,27)sts, 1ch, turn. Work a further 14(14,18,18,18) rows in patt on these sts.

Shape neck

Row 1: patt to last 5sts, 1ch, turn.

Row 2: patt to end, 1ch, turn.

Row 3: patt to last 2sts, dc2tog, 1ch, turn.

Rows 4-5: patt to end.   Fasten off.

BACK

With RS facing miss 1st, join yarn to next st, patt over 43(47,51,55,59)sts, 1ch, turn. Work a further 19(19, 23,23,23)rows in patt on these sts. Fasten off.

LEFT FRONT

With RS facing miss 1st, join yarn to next st, patt to end,1ch,turn.
Work a further 14(14,18,18,18)rows in patt.

Shape neck

Row 1: ss over 5sts, 1ch, patt to end, 1ch, turn.

Row 2: patt to end, 1ch, turn.

Row 3: dc2tog, patt to end, 1ch, turn.

Rows 4-5: patt to end. Fasten off.
With RS tog join shoulder seams.

POCKET LINING

With 5.00mm hook and RS facing, join yarn to first of 15ch of pocket opening, 1ch, 1dc in same place, 14dc,1ch, turn.

Row 2: dc to end, 1ch, turn. Rep last row 13 times.
Fasten off.   Stitch pocket lining to inside of body.

WELT

With RS facing, and 4.50mm hook, join yarn to base of body, 7ch.

Row 1: 1dc in 3rd ch from hook, dc to end, ss to body, 1ss in next base ch,turn.

Row 2: miss 2ss, ss in back loops only, to end, turn.

Row 3: ss in back loops to end, 1ss in body ch, turn.

Row 4: miss 1ss, ss in back loops to end, turn.

Row 5: ss in back loops to end, ss in body ch, 1ss in next base ch,turn.
Rep last 4 rows to edge of other front. Fasten off.

BUTTONHOLE BAND [NB: Right front for girl, left for boy]

With 4.50mm hook and RS facing, join yarn to first st of front. Work dc in row ends of welt to end of centre front, turn.

Row 2: ss in back loops to end, turn.   Rep last row 3 times.   Mark position of 6(6,7,7,7) buttons.

Row 6: [buttonhole row], *ss in back loops to marker, 1ch, miss 1st, rep from * to end, turn.
Row 7: ss in back loops of each st and in chsp to end, turn. Rep row 2 twice. Fasten off.
BUTTONBAND [left for girl, right for boy]
With 4.50mm hook and RS facing, join yarn to first st at front. Work 1dc in each row end and each st across welt and up centre front, turn.
Rep row 2 of buttonhole band 9 times. Fasten off.

HOOD

With 5.50mm hook, make 56(56,60,60,60)ch.
Row 1: 1dc in 3rd ch from hook, dc to end, 1ch, turn. Work patt rows 2-5 as for body until work measures 15(15,18,18,18)cm [6(6,7,7,7)in] or length required ending withWS row, 1ch, turn.
Fold hood in half with WS tog, crochet a crab st through both thicknesses to close centre back seam.
EDGING: With 4.50mm hook and RS facing, work into remaining loops of base ch, dc to end. Fasten off. With RS tog join neck edge of hood and body omitting front bands.

SLEEVES

With 5.50mm hook, make 40(40,48,48,48)ch.
Row 1: 1dc in 3rd ch from hook, dc in each ch to end, 1ch, turn.
Work patt rows 2-5 as body until work measures 12(15,18,21,24)cm [5(6,7,8¼,9½)in] or length required. Fasten off.
CUFFS
With 4.50mm hook and RS facing, join yarn to first st, make 7ch.
Row 1: 1dc in 3rd ch from hook, dc to end, ss to sleeve, 1ss in next ch on sleeve, turn.
Row 2: miss 2ss, ss in back loops to end, turn [6sts]
Row 3: 6ss in back loops only, ss to sleeve, 1ss on sleeve, turn. Last 2 rows form patt. Cont in patt to sleeve end. Fasten off.

TO COMPLETE

With RS tog sew sleeve seams. Sew sleeves into armholes. Sew on buttons to correspond with buttonholes.

[S] WINTER WONDERLAND ***

Materials: 225(250,250,300,300)g DK in White (M): 25(25, 50, 50,50)g in Green: 25(25,50,50,50)g in Red:oddments for bear and rabbit: 4.00mm, 4.50mm and 5.00mm crochet hooks: sequins and beads in varying sizes: 4 black beads (eyes): 2 buttons (back opening).
Size: *To fit chest:* 56(61,66,71,76)cm [22(24,26,28,30)in]
Actual measurement: 64(69,74,79,84)cm [25(27,29,31,33)in]
Back length: 36(38,40,42,42)cm [14¼(15,15¾,16½,16½)in]
Sleeve seam: 23(26,29,32,35)cm [9(10¼,11½,12½,13¾)in]
Tension: 8sts and 9 rows to 5cm [2in] worked in sdc.
Abbreviations: See page 37

FRONT

With 5.00mm hook and M, make 44(48,52,56,60)ch.
Row 1: [RS] 1dc in 2nd ch from hook, dc to end, 1ch, turn.
Row 2: sdc in each st to end, 1ch, turn. Follow chart commencing with the rem 5 rows of border patt. Work 9(13,15,17, 19) rows in sdc. Cont to follow chart in sdc to neck shaping.
SHAPE NECK
Left Side
Row 1: 16(18,19,21,22)sdc, 1ch, turn.
Row 2: sdc2tog, sdc to end, 1ch, turn.
Rows 3 & 4: sdc to end, 1ch, turn. Fasten off.
Right Side
Row 1: miss 8(8,10,10,12)sts, rejoin yarn in next st, 1ch, sdc to end, 1ch, turn.
Row 2: sdc to last 2sts, sdc2tog, 1ch, turn.
Rows 3 & 4: sdc to end, 1ch, turn. Fasten off.

BACK

Work as front for 41(45,47,49,51) rows, omitting tree.

BACK OPENING
First Side
Row 1: 21(23,25,27,29)sdc, 1ch, turn.
Work a further 14 rows on these sts. Fasten off.
Second Side
With RS facing, rejoin yarn to next st.
Row 1: sdc to end, 1ch, turn.
Work a further 14 rows on these sts. Fasten off.

SLEEVES

With 5.00mm hook, make 28ch.
Row 1: 1dc in 3rd ch from hook, dc to end, 1ch, turn
Row 2: 1dc, *3trcl, 1dc, rep from * to end, 1ch, turn
Row 3: dc to end, 1ch, turn. Join in red yarn.
Row 4: 2dc, *3trcl, 1dc, rep from * to last st, 1dc, 1ch, turn. Join in M.
Row 5: 1dc, 2dc in next st, dc to last 2sts, 2dc in next st, 1dc, 1ch, turn [1st inc at both ends of row].
Row 6: As row 2.
Row 7: As row 3. Join in green yarn.
Row 8: As row 4. Join in white yarn.
Row 9: As row 3.
Row 10: As row 2.
Row 11: As row 5.
Cont to work sleeve in patt, inc 1st at each end of every following 6th row and keeping colour changes [3 rows white, 1 row red, 3 rows white, 1 row green] until sleeve measures 19(22,25,28,31)cm [7½(8¾,10, 11¼,12½)in]. Fasten off.
CUFFS
Row 1: With 4.50mm hook and M join to 1st st, 2ch, tr to end, 2ch, turn.
Row 2: 1RtrB, *1RtrF, 1RtrB, rep from * to last st, 1htr, 2ch, turn.
Row 3: 1RtrF, *1RtrB, 1RtrF, rep from * to last st, 1htr, 2ch, turn. Rep last 2 rows once. Fasten off.

WELTS

With 4.50mm hook and M join yarn to first ch of back or front. Work as for cuffs. With RS tog join shoulder seams.

EDGINGS

Back Opening & Neck Edging

With 5.00mm hook, M and WS facing, join yarn to top left back opening, 1ch.

Row 1: 1dc in each row end along opening, 1ch, turn.

Row 2: 1dc in each st along opening and neck, ending at top right back opening, 1ch, turn.

Mark for 2 buttons on band of opening.

Row 3: [buttonhole row] *dc to marker, miss 1st, 1ch, rep from * to end. Fasten off.

Neck Edging Row

With 5.00mm hook, red yarn and RS facing, crab st all round neck. Fasten off.

BEAR

Head: With 4.00mm hook and yarn of chosen colour make 2ch. Do not join but work in continuous rounds.

Rnd 1: 6dc in 2nd ch from hook.

Rnd 2: 2dc in each st.

Rnds 3-5 incl: dc.

Rnd 6: *dc2tog, rep from * to end, ss to join. Pad head lightly with matching yarn.

Rnd 7: Pinch row ends of last rnd tog and work 3dc through both thicknesses evenly across, 1ch, turn.

Body: Row 1:dc to end,1ch,turn.Rep last row 6 times. Fold body in half and join to end of row 7 with ss.

Arms & Legs: [working round body]

Row 1: *4ch, 1dc in 3rd ch from hook, dc to end, **3ss into body, rep from * to **, 1ss into body, rep from * to **, 3ss into body, rep from * to **, 1ss into end of row 7, 1ch, turn.

Row 2: [working round arms, legs and body]: *2dc, 3dc in next st, dc in rem loops of starting ch, ss into body, rep from *ending with 1ss in neck.

Fasten off leaving a tail of yarn for sewing. Pad body and close neck opening.

Muzzle: With 4.00mm hook make 2ch, 6dc in 2nd ch from hook, ss to join. Fasten off. Sew to centre of face.

Ears:[alike] With 4.00mm hook make 2ch, 4tr 1ch 1ss in 2nd ch from hook. Fasten off. Sew to head.

Facial Features: Using black thread, embroider nose and facial features. Attach 2 black beads for eyes.

RABBIT

Head and Body: With 4.00mm hook and yarn of chosen colour, work first 6 rnds as for bear.

Rnd 7: 2dc in each st round.

Rnd 8: dc to end.

Rnd 9: *1dc, 2dc in next st, rep from * to end.

Rnds 10 & 11: As rnd 8.

Rnds 12 & 13: As rnd 9, 1ss. Fasten off.

Pad body lightly. Sew opening closed.

Ears[alike]: With 4.00mm hook make 6ch, 1dc in 2nd ch from hook, 2dc, 1htr, 6htr in last ch, do not turn. Cont along other side of ch with 1htr, dc to end. Fasten off. Sew ears to top of head.

Cheeks: With 4.00mm hook make 2ch, *htr5tog in 2nd ch from hook,** 3ch, rep from * to ** once, 1ch. Fasten off. Sew to face.

Tail: With 5.00mm hook and white yarn, make 2ch, tr6tog in 2nd ch from hook. Fasten off. Sew to body.

Facial Features: With black thread, embroider nose between cheeks and attach 2 black beads for eyes.

TREE DECORATION

Thread small beads onto button thread to make garland. Drape this across the tree and stitch securely in place. Sew on beads and sequins at random.

Sew bear and rabbit securely under tree.

TO COMPLETE

Mark centre stitch on last row of sleeve, match this with shoulder seam, easing sleeve to fit.

With WS facing, join sleeves to body by working through both thicknesses in dc. Fasten off white.

Do not turn work. Join in red yarn, 1ch, crab st to end. Fasten off. With RS tog, join sleeve and side seams.

WINTER WONDERLAND

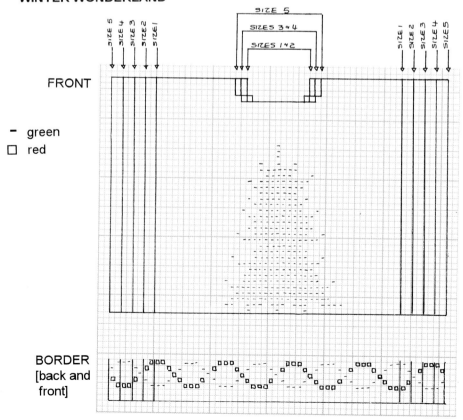

[T] JUNGLE JACKET ***

Materials: -[NB: All quantities refer to DK yarn]

Garment background 450g various shades of green and blue, orange and yellow

Lining, welt & cuffs 450g orange

2 Elephants 50g blue/grey, Oddment of ivory, white felt or funtex, black fabric paint for eyes.

Tiger 25g orange, oddment black, white felt or funtex and black fabric paint for eyes

Lion 25g beige, oddments of black andbrown, 25g beige random for mane, white felt or funtex and black fabric paint for eyes

Large bear 25g tan, oddment of yellow , brown and black, pink emb thread, White felt or funtex and blade fabric paint for eyets

Detachable bear 25g yellow, oddment black, polyester filling, 2 black beads, black embroidery thread, small press stud

Alligator 50g green, oddments of ivory and pink, pale blue emb thread, 2 black beads

Fish Oddment orange, oddment pink, gold embroidery thread, gold metallic thread, 2 black beads

Front bands and branches 25g brown   *Leaves* Oddments of green

Spider Oddment of black or chenille, black emb thread, 2 small beads

Spiders Web Silver metallic thread

Giraffe 25g yellow, oddment black and brown

Small bears Oddments of browns/beige/tan, 2 small balck beades for eyes, black emb thread.

Ladybird Oddments of red and black, 2 small beads for eyes

Rainbow Oddments of purple, pink, blue, green, yellow, orange, red

Monkey Oddments rust and pink, brown emb thread, white felt or funtex and black fabric paint for eyes

Snail Oddments brown and beige

Bee Oddment black DK, yellow emb thread, gold metallic thread, 2 small beads   *Flowers* Oddments yellow and orange

Birds Oddments Black, white and orange, 2 small beads per bird

Mice Oddments pink, brown, beige, DK or chenille, 2 small beads per mouse   *Flowers on tree* Oddment pink

3.00mm, 4.00mm, 4.50mm, 5.00mm crochet hooks; 7 buttons

Actual measurements

(Garment made to fit chest 61-81cm [24-32in])

Chest measurement (actual) 86cm [34in] *Length from shoulder* 51cm[20in]

Sleeve length from shoulder(before adjustable turn up cuff) 33cm[13¼in]

Tension: 8sts and 9 rows to 5cm[2in] measured over shallow dc using a 5.00mm hook.

Abbreviations: See pg 37

BODY

[worked in one piece up to underarms]

NB: Instructions are not given for background colour changes, use as many or as few colours as desired. The background could easily be worked in a single colour.

Background colours: commence with dark shades of green, gradually incorporating paler shades of green and blue as work progresses. Follow chart for colour changes. Instructions are given for garment shaping, (ie armholes and neck edge), which can be easily adjusted by reading the chart.

Begin at lower edge of garment with 5.00mm hook.

Row 1: Make 131ch, 1dc in 2nd ch from hook dc to end, turn. [first row on chart].

Row 2: 1ch, sdc to end, turn. Rep row 2 48 times.
Divide for armhole.

RIGHT FRONT

Row 51: 1ch, patt for 31sts, turn.

Row 52: 1ch, patt to end, turn.

Row 53: 1ch, patt to last 2sts, sdc2tog, turn.

Rows 54 & 55: 1ch, patt to end, turn.

Row 56: 1ch, sdc2tog, patt to end, turn.

Rows 57 & 58: 1ch, patt to end, turn.

Rep rows 53-58 incl twice more

Work rows 53-55 incl once.

Row 74: 1ch, sdc2tog, patt to end, turn.

Row 75: ss over 7sts, patt to end, turn. [17sts].

Row 76: 1ch, patt to last 2sts, sdc2tog, turn.

Row 77: 1ch, patt to last 2sts, sdc2tog, turn.

Row 78: 1ch, patt to last 2sts, sdc2tog, turn.

Rows 79-81 incl: 1ch, sdc to end. Fasten off.

BACK

Row 51: With RS facing miss 1st, rejoin yarn to next st, 1sdc, 65sdc, turn [66sts].

Row 52: 1ch, patt to end, turn.

Row 53: 1ch, sdc2tog, patt to last 2sts, sdc2tog, turn.

Rows 54 & 55: 1ch, sdc T end, turn.

Rep rows 53-55 incl 8 times.

Row 80: 1ch, sdc to end, turn.

Row 81: 1ch, sdc to end. Fasten off.

LEFT FRONT

Row 51: With RS facing, miss 1st, rejoin yarn to next st, 1sdc, sdc in each st to end, turn. [31sts]

Row 52: 1ch, patt to end, turn.

Row 53: 1ch, sdc2tog, patt to end, turn.

Rows 54 & 55: 1ch, sdc to end, turn.

Row 56: 1ch, patt to last 2sts, sdc2tog, turn.

Rows 57 & 58: 1ch, sdc to end, turn.

Rep rows 53-58 incl twice more.

Rep rows 53-55 incl once, turn.

Row 74: 1ch, sdc in each st to last 2sts, sdc2tog, turn.

Row 75: 1ch, 17sdc, turn.

Row 76: 1ch, sdc2tog, patt to end, turn.

Row 77: 1ch, sdc2tog, patt to end, turn.

Row 78: 1ch, sdc2tog, patt to end, turn.

Rows 79-81 incl: 1ch, sdc in each st to end, turn.
Fasten off.

HOOD

[Commence at face edge of hood]

Background colours: worked in shades of yellow and orange around yellow sun, shading to pale blues and greens towards sides of hood.

Row 1: Make 71ch, 1dc in 2nd ch from hook, dc to end, turn. [1st row of chart].

Row 2: 1ch, sdc to end, turn. Rep row 2 29 times.
Do not fasten off. Fold hood in half and crab st centre back seam tog on RS.   Fasten off.

Rainbow

Row 1: With RS facing, rejoin purple yarn to first st of hood at face edge with ss, ss to end, turn. Fasten off.

Row 2: Join in pink, ss in back loops to end, turn.
Fasten off.

Row 3: Join in blue, ss in back loops to end, turn.
Cont fastening off and joining in new colour on each row for green, yellow, orange and red. Fasten off

Next row: With RS facing, join colour chosen for welts and/or cuffs to first st of face edge. Work ss into back loops to end, turn.

EDGING

ss in back loops of first 4sts, *3ch, ss into 3rd ch from hook, ss into next 3sts, rep from * to end. Fasten off.

SLEEVES

Background colours: worked in shades of blue and green,, shading as for back and front of garment. Number of sts and sleeve shaping aresame for both sleeves, however follow separate charts for colour changes for the animals.

[NB: The Alligator sleeve background is worked in sdc. The Alligator (indicated on chart by a 'dot') is a dtr worked only on WS rows. The two centre 'dots' down centre back of alligator are crossed double trebles.

Row 1: Make 51ch, 1dc in 2nd ch from hook, dc to end, turn. [first row of chart].

Row 2: 1ch, sdc to end, turn. Rep last row 28 times, turn.

Rows 31-34 incl: 1ch, sdc2tog, sdc to last 2sts, sdc2tog, turn.

Row 35: 1ch, sdc to end, turn.

Rows 36-40 incl: as rows 31-35

Rows 41-43 incl: 1ch, sdc2tog, sdc to last 2sts, sdc2tog, turn.

Row 44: 1ch, sdc to end, turn.

Row 45: 1ch, sdc2tog, sdc to last 2sts, sdc2tog, turn. Rep last 2 rows 3 times more.

Row 52: 1ch, sdc in each st to end, turn.

Row 53: ss in first 2sts, sdc to last 2sts, ss in next sdc, turn.

Row 54: miss ss, ss into next sdc, sdc to last st, ss in last sdc and ss into next ss, turn.

Row 55: 1ch, miss 2ss, ss in next st, sdc in each st to last 2sdc, ss in last 2sdc. Fasten off.

ASSEMBLING THE GARMENT

When the garment is complete piece the sections together. Mice, bugs, leaves, etc, can be sewn to the garment at any stage,but the task is simplified if garment sections are flat, exceptions being the animals/bird to be attached to the shoulder seam, and the alligator head.
With RS facing, join shoulder seams.
Place a marker at centre back neck edge and match with centre back neck edge of hood. Match centre front of garment with row ends of hood face edge. Sew tog. Front band is added later. Sew approx 2.5cm[1in] of underarm sleeve seam. Insert sleeves into armholes, matching shoulder seam with centre st of sleeve.

LEFT FRONT BAND

With 4.50mm hook join brown yarn [or tree trunk colour yarn] to left front neck edge, 1ss in each row end to end, turn. [75sts]

Row 2: ss in front loops to end, turn.
Rep last row 6 times more. Fasten off.

RIGHT FRONT BAND

Join yarn to lower right front and work 1ss in each row end up to neck edge, turn.[75sts]

Row 2: ss in front loops to end, turn.
Rep row 2 3 times more.

Row 6 [buttonhole row]: using front loops only work 2ss, 2ch, miss 2sts, *11ss, 2ch, miss 2sts, rep from * 4 times, ss to end, turn. [6 buttonholes made, the 7th buttonhole will be made in the welt].

Row 7: working in front loops only *ss to 2ch sp, 2ss in 2chsp, rep from * to end, turn.

Row 8: ss in front loops to end. Do not turn.

Row 9: Crab st to end, cont working crab st along top edge of band. Fasten off.

CUFFS

With 4.00mm hook, orange yarn and RS facing, join yarn to first base ch of sleeve, dc to end. [50sts]. Fasten off.

Row 1: Rejoin yarn to first st made on last row with a ss. Make 16ch, ss in 2nd ch from hook, ss to end [15sts]. ss into next 2sts on sleeve, turn.

Row 2 Miss last 2ss, ss in back loops to end, turn.

Row 3 ss in back loops to end, ss into next 2sts on sleeve, turn. Rep rows 2 and 3 to end. Fasten off.
Sew rem of underarm sleeve and cuff seam.

WELT

With 4.00mm hook, and RS facing, join orange yarn to lower left front, dc along base ch. Fasten off.

Row 1: join yarn to left front band with ss, make 9ch, ss in 2nd ch from hook, ss to end, ss into each of next 2sts on band, turn.

Row 2: miss last ss, ss in back loops to end, turn.

Row 3: ss in back loops to end, ss in each of next 2dc, turn.

Row 4: miss last ss made, ss in back loops to end, turn.

Row 5: ss in back loops to end, ss in next dc, turn.
Rep rows 2-5 incl until 2dc rem on base ch, turn.

Next row: 3ss in back loops, 2ch, miss 2sts, ss in back loops to end, turn.[1 buttonhole made] *ss in back loops, 2ss in 2chsp, rep from * to end, finishing with RS facing, ss into last dc made on base ch. Fasten off.

LINING OF GARMENT

With 5.00mm hook and chosen yarn, work in sdc. Follow patt for front, back and sleeves exactly as for outer garment, omitting colour changes. Work hood as for outer hood omitting colour changes and patt rows for rainbow. Work 4 rows sdc to replace rainbow band. Sew centre back seam.
Assemble lining as for outer garment.
Insert lining into jacket placing WS tog and carefully hand sew round edges of body, hood, and lower edges of sleeves.
Sew points of hood tog invisibly to hold in place.

POCKET LINING [2 alike]

Row 1: With 5.00mm hook and work upside-down, join chosen yarn to underside of 18ch made on pocket opening row with 1dc, dc to end.

Row 2: 1ch, sdc to end, turn.
Rep last row 28 times. Fasten off.
Fold pocket lining in half and catch stitches from last row to inside edge of pocket opening. Sew side seams tog and stitch fold of pocket to main body of jacket.

POCKET OPENING [2 alike]

With 5.00mm hook, appropriate colour, and RS of work facing, join yarn to left st on pocket opening row with 1dc, work crab st to end. Fasten off.

ADDITIONAL FEATURES

LARGE ELEPHANT

Ears: [2 alike]
With 5.00mm hook and blue/grey yarn to match head, commence work at base of ear, 10ch,

Row 1: 2dc in 2nd ch from hook *dc in next ch, 2dc in next ch, rep from * to end, turn.

Row 2: 1ch, dc in each st to end, turn.

Row 3: 1ch, 2dc in first st, 2dc, (2dc in next st, 2dc)3 times, 1dc, 2dc in next st, turn.

Rows 4 & 5: 1ch, dc to end, turn.

Row 6: 1ch, miss 1st st, dc to last 2sts, dc2tog, turn.

Rep last row 5 times more, ss into next st on last row. Fasten off.

With RS facing join yarn to last st at base of ear, work 1 row dc round outer edge of ear placing 1dc in each row end and 1dc into each dc along ear tip. Do not turn.

1ch, crab st round all 3 edges of ear. Fasten off.

Sew ears in position at 5th row down from top of head.

Trunk

With 4.50mm hook and blue/grey yarn, commence work at tip of trunk.

Rnd 1: 2ch, 6dc in 2nd ch from hook, do not join unless otherwise stated.

Rnd 2: dc in back loops to end. Rep rnd 2 3 times.

Rnd 6: *2dc in next st, 2dc, rep from * to end [8sts]

Rnd 7: dc to end.

Rnd 8: *2dc in next st, 3dc, rep from * to end, [10sts]

Rnd 9: dc to end.

Rnd 10: *2dc in next st, 4dc, rep from *to end [12sts]

Rnd 11: dc to end, ss into next st, turn.

Rnd 12: 1ch, miss first st, 6dc, ss into next st, turn.

Rnd 13: miss first st, 5dc, ss into next st, turn.

Rnd 14: miss first st, 4dc, ss into next st, turn.

Rnd 15: miss first st, 3dc, ss into next st, do not turn.

Rnd 16: 1ch, 1dc in each row end, ss into next st.

Fasten off. Pad trunk lightly and sew to face of elephant just below centre, with trunk pointing downwards.

Tusks: [2 alike]

Rnd 1: With 4.50mm hook and ivory yarn, 2ch, 4dc in 2nd ch from hook, do not join.

Rnd 2: 2dc in each st to end.

Rnd 3: dc to end. Rep last rnd 3 times, ss into next st of last rnd. Fasten off. Pad lightly and gather opening closed. Sew one tusk to each side of trunk.

Eyes:

Trace over sketch and use as a template to, cut 2 eyes from white felt or funtex and add eye detail using black fabric paint.

Sew eyes in position just above trunk, leaving a 2cm [¾in] gap between. With black yarn, embroider eyebrow detail.

SMALL ELEPHANT

Ears: [2 alike]

Row 1: With 5.00mm hook and blue/grey yarn, commence at base of ear, 8ch, 2dc in 2nd ch from hook, *dc in next ch, 2dc in next ch, rep from * to end, turn.

Row 2: 1ch, dc to end, turn.

Row 3: 1ch, 2dc in first st,*(2dc, 2dc in next st) twice, 3dc, 2dc in last st, turn.

Row 4: 1ch, 2dc in first st, *2dc, 2dc in next st, rep from * to end, turn.

Row 5 1ch, dc2tog, dc to last 2sts, dc2tog, turn.

Rep last row 6 times more. Fasten off.

With RS facing, join yarn to last st at base of ear, dc round outer edge of ear, do not turn. 1ch, crab st round all 3 edges of ear. Fasten off. Commencing on 5th row down from top of head, sew ears to elephant. Fold top of ear down and catch sew in place.

Trunk

Work as for large elephant trunk until end of rnd 6. Omit rnds 7-13 incl. Work from rnd 14, to end.

Eyes

As for large elephant leaving only 1.25cm [½in gap]

LARGE BEAR [on left front]

Hands [Make 2 alike]

With 4.00mm hook and yarn to match body, work in cont spiralling rnds unless otherwise stated.

Rnd 1: 2ch, 6dc in 2nd ch from hook.

Rnd 2: 2dc in each st around [12sts].

Rnd 3: *1dc, 2dc in next st, rep from * to end. Join with ss into top of first dc of round [18sts].

Rnd 4: 1ch, 2dc, 5tr in next st, drop loop from hook and insert hook into top of first tr of group and pull loop through [thumb made], 15dc.

Rnd 5: dc, miss thumb, dc to end [17sts]

Rnd 6: 1dc, (dc2tog) twice, 4dc, dc2tog, 6dc [14sts].

Rnd 7: 6dc, (dc2tog) twice, 4dc [12sts]

Rnd 8: dc2tog to end, [6sts], ss into top of first st of round to join. Fasten off. Sew opening closed. Sew hands in place - one around centre, positioning to end of wrist, and the other to the remaining arm, pointing towards face slightly.

Feet [Make 2 alike]

With 4.00mm hook, commence with contrasting yarn.

Rnd 1: 2ch, 8dc in 2nd ch from hook, join with ss into top of first st. Fasten off contrast. Change to main and join to any st with 1dc.

Rnd 2: dc in same st as last dc, dc to end [16sts]

Rnd 3: 1ch, *1dc, 2dc in next st, rep from * to end [24sts]. Join with ss into top of first st of round.

Rnd 4: 1ch, working into back loop of sts, dc in first dc, (dc2tog)3 times. *4tr in next st, drop loop from hook and insert hook into top of first tr of group and pull through [toe made], 2dc, rep from *3 times, (dc2tog) twice, dc in last st. Join with a ss.

Rnd 5: 1ch,[missing toes], dc2tog to end. Do not join.

Rnd 6: (dc2tog)3 times, ss into next st. Fasten off.

Sew feet to garment just below lower body, leaving a 2.5cm[1in] gap between each foot.

Ears: (Make 2 alike)

Inner: With 4.50mm hook and contrast commence at base of ear, 2ch,1dc 5tr 1dc in 2nd ch from hook, turn

Row 2: 1ch,1dc in first dc, *2dc in next st,1dc, rep from * to end. Fasten off contrast.

Outer: Commencing at base of ear with yarn to match head and body, rep rows 1 and 2 of inner ear, do not fasten off after last row.

Row 3: Holding inner and outer ear pieces with WS tog, work 2dc in each st to end, do not turn. Cont to work along base of ear by working 5dc evenly across, join with a ss into top of first st of round. Fasten off. Sew to head, leaving a gap of approx 1¾in between.

Muzzle:

Rnd 1: With 4.50 hook and yarn to match body, 2ch, 6dc in 2nd ch from hook. Do not join rounds unless otherwise stated.

Rnd 2: 2dc in each st to end [12sts]

Rnd 3: *1dc, 2dc in next st, rep from * to end [18sts]

Rnd 4: *2dc in next st, 2dc in next st, rep from * to end [24sts]

Rnd 5: dc to end.

Rnd 6: dc to end, ss into next st. Fasten off.

Nose: With dark brown yarn, embroider nose onto muzzle at centre, shaping it slightly.

Tongue:

With 3.00mm hook and pink emb thread, 6ch, 1dc in 2nd ch from hook, dc to last ch, 4dc in last ch, do not turn. Cont to work along other edge of base ch, dc in each st to end. Fasten off.

Sew tongue to muzzle, approx 1.25cm [½in] below nose. Sew muzzle to lower part of face of bear, padding lightly before closing opening.

LION

Mane: Using a double strand of DK yarn (ie 2 balls of contrasting colour) and 5.00mm hook join yarn to any st on outer head with 1dc, pull up a 3.5cm[1½in] loop of yarn, 2ch, *1dc in next st, pull up a loop of yarn, 2ch, 1dc, rep from *round face. Work a further 2rnds the same. Fasten off.

Cheeks: Using yarn to match body, make two 2.5cm [1in] dia. pom-poms. Sew pom-poms side by side to face, leaving a small gap between.

Snout: With 4.50mm hook and black yarn, commence at lower point of snout.

Rnd 1: 2ch, 4dc in 2nd ch from hook.
Do not join rnds unless otherwise stated.

Rnd 2: 2dc in each st to end [8sts]

Rnd 3: dc to end.

Rnd 4: *1dc, 2dc in next st, rep from *to end, ss in next st. Fasten off. Fold snout in half and close opening. Position snout on face just slightly above, but between cheeks and sew in place. Before fastening off, continue to embroider facial features.

Ears: [2 alike]

Work as for ears of large bear. Sew to head positioning bet rnds 2 and 3 of mane, leaving a 9cm[3½in] gap.

Tail: With 4.50mm hook and yarn to match lion, leave a small length of yarn before commencing to attach to lion: 4ch, join with ss, dc to end of round, do not join unless otherwise stated. Cont to work in unjoined rnds until tail measures approx 9.5cm[3¾in], ss into next st. Fasten off.

Tip of tail: With yarn to match mane, wind yarn several times around a 3cm [1¼in] wide piece of card. Slip yarn off and wrap another length of yarn round the folded yarn approx 0.5cm[¼in] from the end to make a tassel. Sew this to the tail. Sew body end of tail to body of lion just above legs, tucking it under mane to conceal the end. Curl tail upwards slightly and sew into position.

Eyes:

Using sketch as a guide, cut two eyes from white felt or funtex and paint eye detail with black fabric paint. Sew eyes in place just above cheeks.

SMALL BEARS FACES

Snout

With 4.50mm hook and yarn to match each bear:
3ch, 6htr into 3rd ch from hook, ss into first htr to join. Fasten off. The WS of fabric is RS of work. Sew snout to face of bear just below centre of face. With black DK yarn or black chenille, embroider nose onto snout. With a single strand of black embroidery thread, embroider bear facial features directly under nose.

Ears: [2 alike]

3ch, 5htr ss into 3rd ch from hook. Fasten off. Sew ears to head, approx 2.5cm[1in] apart. Attach 2 small beads for eyes.

TIGER

Ears [2 alike]

Inner: With 4.50mm hook work as inner ear of large bear.

Outer:

Row 1: as row 1 of inner ear, do not fasten off orange yarn.

Row 2: 1ch, 1dc in first st, *2dc in next, 1dc, rep from * to end, do not fasten off.

Row 3: Holding inner and outer ear pieces with WS tog, 1ch, [crochet through both pieces] 2dc in each st to end, do not turn, cont along base of ear working 5dc evenly across. Join with a ss into top of first st of round. Fasten off.

Sew to top of head, leaving 4cm[1¾in] gap between.

Cheeks [2 alike]

With orange yarn make two 2.5cm[1in] dia pom-poms. Sew side by side to face, leaving a small gap between.

Snout

4.00mm hook and black yarn, commencing at lower point of snout:

Rnd 1: 2ch, 4dc in 2nd ch from hook, do not turn unless otherwise stated.

Rnd 2: 2dc in each st to end [8sts].

Rnd 3: dc to end.

Rnd 4: dc to end, ss into next st. Fasten off leaving a tail of yarn. Fold nose in half and sew opening closed. Place snout centrally on face, slightly above and between cheeks and sew in place. Before fastening off continue to embroider facial features.

Eyes

Using sketcha as a template cut two pieces from white felt or funtex and paint eye detail with black fabric paint. Sew to face just above cheeks.

Tail

With 4.00mm hook, commence with orange yarn. Do not join rounds unless otherwise stated.

Rnd 1: 2ch, 6dc in 2nd ch from hook.

Rnd 2: dc to end.

Rnd 3: Join in black yarn, dc to end.

Rnd 4: Join in orange yarn, dc to end.

Rep rows 3 & 4 until tail measures approx 17.5cm[7in] ss into next st. Fasten off.

Sew one end of the tail to just inside corner of pocket.

ALLIGATOR

Inner Jaws

Row 1: With 4.50mm hook and pink yarn 5ch, 1dc in 2nd ch from hook, dc to end, turn.

Rows 2 & 3: 1ch, dc to end, turn.

Row 4: 1ch, 2dc, 2dc in next st, dc in last st, turn.

Row 5: 1ch, 2dc, 2dc in next st, dc to end, turn.

Rows 6-9: 1ch, 3dc, 2dc in next st, dc to end, turn.

Row 10: 1ch, 3dc, dc2tog, dc to end, turn.

Row 11: 1ch, 2dc, dc2tog, dc to end, turn.

Row 12 1ch, 2dc, dc2tog, dc in last st, turn.

Row 13: 1ch, dc to end, turn.

Rep last row twice more. Fasten off.

Lower Jaws: With 4.50mm hook and green yarn, work as first 9 rows of inner jaws. Fasten off.

Upper Jaws:

Row 1: With 4.50mm hook and green yarn, 5ch, dc in 2nd ch from hook and each ch to end, turn.

Row 2: 1ch, (1dc tr3tog) in first st, 1dc, tr3tog, 1dc, turn

Row 3: [RS], 1ch, 2dc, 1dc, miss next tr3tog, dc in last st, turn.

Row 4: 1ch, 2dc, 2dc in next st, 1sdc in last st, turn.

Row 5: As row 4.

Row 6: 3dc, 2dc in next st, dc to end, turn.

Row 7: As row 6.

Row 8: 1ch, 4dc, 2dc in next st, dc to end, do not turn

Row 9: With WS of upper and inner jaw pieces tog and inner mouth facing, match shaping, work 1dc at each row end and 2dc in corners to end of lower jaw, ss into first dc of round, do not fasten off.

Head: Cont working in green yarn along top edge of upper jaw.

Row 1: 1ch, 2dc in each st to end of upper jaw, 1dc in each st of lower jaw, ss into top of first st of round, turn

Row 2: 1ch, dc into each st of lower jaw [9sts], 1dc, 2dc in next st, dc to last 2sts, 2dc in next st, 1dc in last st, ss into top of first st to join, turn.

Row 3: 1ch, 2dc in first st, dc to last 2sts of upper jaw, 2dc in next st, 1dc in each st of lower jaw, ss to join. Do not turn. Work in cont rounds, do not join unless otherwise stated.

Rnds 4 & 5: dc to end.

Rnd 6: 3dc, (dc2tog, 3dc)3 times, dc to end.

Rnd 7: 3dc, dc2tog, 1dc, dc2tog, dc to end.

Rnd 8: 2dc, dc2tog, 5dc, dc2tog, dc to end.

Rnd 9: 1dc, dc2tog, 4dc, dc2tog, dc to end.

Rnd 10: 2dc, dc2tog, 1dc, dc2tog, dc to end.

Rnd 11: (dc2tog, 2dc)twice, dc2tog, dc to end, ss into next st to join. Fasten off green.

Teeth With 4.00mm hook and white or cream yarn, work into back loops of rnd 9 where upper and lower jaws are joined to inner jaw: Join yarn to lower jaw with a ss *ss in next st, 2ch, dc in 2nd ch from hook, ss in next st, rep from * along lower jaws, ss into first st of upper jaw, **ss into next st, 2ch, dc in 2nd ch from hook, ss into next st, rep from ** around upper jaw, ss into first dc of round. Fasten off white. Pad head lightly but do not fill the jaws. Gather opening closed at back head. After cuff has been worked on this sleeve, sew head in position to body.

Eye Socket [2 alike]

With 4.50mm hook and green yarn, do not join, but work in cont rnds.

Rnd 1: 2ch, 6dc in 2nd ch from hook [6sts]

Rnd 2: *2dc in next st, 1dc, rep from * to end [9sts]

Rnd 3: dc to end.

Rnd 4: As rnd 3, ss into next st. Fasten off.

Pad lightly, gather and close opening.

Sew to head position between rows 1 & 2.

Nostrils: Using black yarn, sew in nostrils.

Eyes: [2 alike]

With 3.00mm hook and pale blue embroidery thread make 3ch, 10htr in 3rd ch from hook. Fasten off. Sew to centre front of eye socket. Attach a small black bead to centre of each eye.

Legs: [4 alike] With 4.50mm hook and green yarn, [NB: leave a small end of yarn before commencing to sew to body] commence at body end of leg:

Rnd 1: 2ch, 8dc in 2nd ch from hook.

Do not join but work in cont rnds.

Rnd 2: 2dc in each st to end [16sts]

Rnd 3-5 incl: dc to end.

Rnd 6: (3dc, dc2tog)3 times, 1dc [13sts]

Rnd 7: dc to end.

Rnd 8: (2dc, dc2tog)3 times, 1dc [10sts]

Rnd 9: dc to end.

Rep last row 3 times. Do not fasten off. Pad lightly.

Rnd 13: (3dc, dc2tog)twice [8sts] ss in next st.

Rnd 14: Pinch end together. Crochet the two layers tog with 3dc, turn.

Rnd 15: 1ch, 2dc in first st, 1dc, 2dc in next st [5sts].

Rnd 16: Form toes (1ch, tr3tog in same st)4 times, ss into same st as last st. Fasten off.

Back legs: Sew to body approx 12.5cm[5in] down from tip of tail and bend legs slightly to form shaping. Sew in place.

Front legs: Sew to body approx 10cm[4in] down from back legs, shaping as before.

SMALL MOUSE [Make as few or as many of these as desired - they can be attached anywhere on the jacket]. For DK yarn use a 4.00mm hook and for chenille use a 4.50mm hook. [NB:WS of work is RS].

Tail

Make a 7.5cm[3in] length of single twisted cord and set aside. Make a large knot in the body end of tail.

Head and Body

Do not join rnds unless otherwise stated.

Rnd 1: 3ch, 8dc in 3rd ch from hook.

Rnd 2: Work in cont rnds 18dc. Slip tail through centre 'ring' of mouse making sure the knot of the tail is does not pull through, (dc2tog, 1dc)twice, (dc2tog)5 times. Fasten off.

Ears

3ch, 1dc 3tr 1ss in 2nd ch from hook, 1dc 3tr 1ss in last ch. Fasten off. Sew ears to centre of head, approx 1.25cm [½in] from tip of nose. Attach 2 small beads for eyes.

MEDIUM MOUSE

[Make whatever number desired - they can be attached anywhere the jacket] DK yarn use 4.00mm hook, for chenille use a 4.50mm hook. [NB: WS of work is RS]

Tail

Make a 10cm[4in] length of single twisted cord and set aside. Make a large knot in the body end of tail.

Head and Body

Do not join rnds unless otherwise stated.

Rnd 1: 3ch, 8dc in 3rd ch from hook.

Rnd 2: (2dc in next st, 1dc)4 times.

Rnd 3 & part of 4: work 32dc without shaping. Slip tail through centre 'ring' of mouse, making sure the knot does not pull through.

Rnd 4: (dc2tog, 2dc in next 2sts)8times, (dc2tog) twice, ss in next st. Fasten off.

Ears

Row 1: 3ch, 1dc 1tr 2dtr 1tr 1ss in 2nd ch from hook, 1dc 1tr 2dtr 1tr 1ss in next ch. Fasten off. Sew ears to centre of head, approx 1-2cm[½-¾in] from tip of nose. Attach 2 small beads for eyes.

FISH

Inner Mouth

Row 1: With 4.00mm hook and pink yarn make 2ch, 6dc in 2nd ch from hook, ss into top of first dc. Fasten off and set aside.

Head

With 4.00mm hook and orange yarn, commence at body end of fish. 18ch, ss into first st to form a ring. Do not join unless otherwise stated, work in cont rnds.

Rnd 1: dc in each ch [18sts])
Rnd 2: *4dc, dc2tog rep from * to end [15sts]
Rnd 3: dc to end.
Rnd 4: *3dc, dc2tog, rep from * to end [12sts]
Rnd 5: dc to end.
Rnd 6: *2dc, dc2tog rep from * to end [9sts]
Rnd 7: dc to end, ss into next st. Fasten off.
With WS tog insert inner mouth into head and sew to back loops of last rnd of head.
Fasten off.

Mouth

With 4.00mm hook and orange yarn, join to any front loop of last row, row crab st to end, ss to join.Fasten off

Fins [2 alike]

Row 1: With 4.00mm hook and orange yarn make 6ch, 1htr in 3rd ch from hook, 2dc, 3dc in next ch, do not turn - cont working along base ch, 1dc 2htr 1tr in end ch. Fasten off.

Eyes [2 alike]

Row 1: With 3.00mm hook, gold embroidery thread and gold metallic thread tog make 2ch 8dc in 2nd ch from hook, ss into first st. Fasten off.

Assembling Fish

Sew fish to alligator sleeve, just above an alligator's rear leg, padding lightly before sewing opening closed. Sew a fin to each side of the fish. Sew eyes to fish, approx 2 rows down from mouth.

Tail

Row 1: With 4.00mm hook and orange yarn make 4ch, 1dc in 2nd ch from hook, 2dc [3sts] turn.
Row 2: 1ch, 1dc in first st, 2dc in next st, 1dc in last st, turn (4)
Row 3: *5ch, 1dc in 2nd ch from hook, 1htr, 2tr, ss into next 2sts, rep from * once more. Fasten off. Sew tail to alligator sleeve approx 1.25cm[½in] above fish body.

SNAIL

Make as many or as few as desired. [Use 4.00mm hook throughout]

Body

Row 1: With beige yarn make 6ch, ss in 2nd ch from hook and each ch to end. Fasten off and set aside.

Shell

First half: With brown yarn make 2ch, 6dc in 2nd ch from hook, ss to join. Fasten off and set aside.

Second half: Make as for first half but do not fasten off. Place the 2 shell pieces with WS tog and with yarn ends tucked in, ss round the shell pieces using each st. Fasten off. Sew shell centrally to body. Attach completed snails to garment, one to the alligator back and the other to a leaf on the tiger pocket.

MONKEY

Ears [2 alike]

With 4.50mm hook and yarn to match body make 2ch, 5htr 1ss in 2nd ch from hook. Fasten off. Sew an ear to either side of the head.

Lower Face

Row 1: With 4.50mm hook and pink yarn to match face make 4ch, dc in 2nd ch from hook, 1dc, 3dc in next ch. Do not turn.
Row 2: Cont to work along other edge of base ch, 1dc, 2dc in next st, ss into top of first dc of rnd to join.
Rnd 3: dc to end, ss to join.
Rnd 4: *1dc, 2dc in next st, rep from * to end. Fasten off.

Facial Features

Using a double strand of brown embroidery thread, embroider mouth and nostrils to lower face. Sew lower face to head of monkey, padding lightly before sewing opening closed.

Tail

With 4.00mm hook and yarn to match body make 30ch, ss in 2nd ch from hook and each ch to end. Fasten off. Sew to monkey.

Eyes

Using patt, cut two eyes from white felt or funtex and paint eye detail with black fabric paint. Sew to monkey directly above nostrils.

GIRAFFE

Head

Rnd 1: With 4.50mm hook and yellow yarn to match body make 2ch, 6dc in 2nd ch from hook. Do not join but work in cont rnds.
Rnd 2: 2dc in each st to end [12sts]
Rnd 3: *1dc, 2dc in next st, rep from * to end [18sts]
Rnd 4-10 incl: dc to end.
Rnd 11: *dc2tog, 1dc, rep from * to end [12sts] Pad lightly.
Rnd 12: dc2tog to end, ss into next st. Fasten off.

Snout

Rnd 1: With 4.00mm hook and yellow yarn make 2ch, 6dc in 2nd ch from hook.Do not join but work in cont rnds.
Rnd 2: 2dc in each st to end [12sts]
Rnd 3: dc to end. Fasten off.
With black yarn, embroider nose onto centre of snout. With a single strand of red embroidery thread, embroider mouth. Attach snout to head, padding lightly before sewing opening closed.

Ears [2 alike]

Rnd 1: with 4.50mm hook and yellow yarn make 6ch, 1dc in 2nd ch from hook, 2dc, 1htr, 7tr in next ch. Do not turn but cont working along other edge of base ch, 1htr, 3dc. Do not turn.
Rnd 2: 1ch, crab st to end. Fasten off.
Sew to side of head approx 2.5cm[1in] apart.

Horns [2 alike]

Row 1: With 4.00mm hook and yellow yarn make 4ch, ss into 2nd ch from hook and each ch to end. Fasten off. Sew side by side centrally between ears.

Eyes Using black yarn, embroider eyes to head, just above snout. Highlight each eye using a double strand of white embroidery thread.

Attaching to Garment

Position assembled head onto jacket shoulder, aligning with neck of giraffe and sew securely in place.

BIRD - STANDING

With 4.50mm hook and cream yarn throughout

Head and Body [NB: Bird is worked inside-out. Do not join rnds but work in cont rnds unless otherwise stated].

Rnd 1: 2ch, 8dc in 2nd ch from hook.

Rnd 2-4 incl: dc to end. After 4th rnd pad head lightly

Rnd 5: (dc2tog)4 times [4sts]

Rnd 6: 2dc to end [8sts]

Rnd 7: *1dc, 2dc in next st, rep from * to end [12sts]

Rnd 8: dc to end.

Rnd 9: 1dc, 2dc in next st, rep from * to end [16sts]

Rnd 10: As rnd 8.

Rnd 11: dc2tog to end [8sts]. Pad lightly.

Rnd 12: dc2tog to end [4sts], ss into next st. Fasten off

Wings [2 alike]

3ch, dc in 2nd ch from hook, 1dc 1htr 3tr 1htr 1dc in next ch. Do not turn, cont to work in other edge of base ch, 1dc,1ss. Fasten off. Sew a wing to each side of body

Tail

Wind yarn around 3 fingers approx 4 times, fold loops in half and tie tog in a figure of eight shape with another piece of yarn. Sew to lower section of back of bird, approx 0.5cm[¼in] from base.

Beak

With 4.50mm hook and orange yarn, 2ch, dc in 2nd ch from hook. Fasten off. Sew beak centrally to front of head, attach 2 beads on faceabove beak for the eyes

BIRD FLYING [2 alike]

With 4.50mm hook and black yarn make as for standing bird, omitting 4th rnd. Pad head only - not body. Sew beak and eyes to head at an angle.

DETACHABLE TEDDY [in pocket With 4.50mm

hook and yellow yarn, work bear inside-out, do not turn but work in cont rnds unless otherwise stated:

Head and Body

Rnd 1: 2ch, 6dc in 2nd ch from hook.

Rnd 2: *2dc in next st, 1dc, rep from * to end [9sts]

Rnd 3: As 2, but 2dc in last st [15sts]

Rnd 4: 2dc, 2dc in next st rep from * to end [20sts]

Rnd 5-8 incl: dc to end.

Rnd 9: *3dc, dc2tog, rep from * to end [16sts]

Rnd 10: *2dc, dc2tog, rep from * to end [12sts]

Rnd 11: *1dc, dc2tog, rep from * to end [8sts] Pad head lightly.

Rnd 12: 2dc in each st to end [16sts]

Rnd 13:*1dc, 2dc in next st, rep from * to end [24sts]

Rnd 14-18 incl: dc in each st to end.

Rnd 19: 4dc, dc2tog, rep from * to end [20sts]

Rnd 20: *3dc, dc2tog, rep from * to end [16sts]

Rnd 21: *2dc, dc2tog, rep from * to end [12sts], ss in next st. Fasten off. Pad lightly and sew opening closed.

Arms & Legs [4 alike]

Rnd 1: 2ch, 8dc in 2nd ch from hook.

Rnd 2: dc in each st to end [8sts] Rep last rnd 5 times After last rnd, ss in next st. Fasten off.

Assembling Position arms at body sides, close to neck and sew securely in place. Position legs at end of body,

approx 1.25cm[½in] apart and sew in place.

Muzzle

Rnd 1: 2ch, 6dc in 2nd ch from hook.

Rnd 2: 2dc in each st to end [12sts]

Rnd 3: dc to end, ss in next st. Fasten off. With black yarn, embroider nose to centre of muzzle. Using a double strand of embroidery thread, embroider facial features under nose. Sew muzzle to lower half of head padding lightly before sewing opening closed. Attach a black bead for each eye, just above muzzle. Sew press stud to bears upper left arm and the other half of the press stud to the large bears hand. Position bear inside pocket. Close press stud to hold in place.

Ears [2 alike]

Make 3ch, 9tr in 3rd ch from hook. Fasten off. Sew to sides of head.

SPIDERS WEB

With silver metallic thread, embroider web on right front, between tiger and small bear, positioning centre of web level with edge of front band.

Commence by embroidering curves and then add the 'straight lines' [see diagram on pg000].

SPIDER

Body

With 4.50mm hook and blackDK or chenille yarn make 3ch, tr6tog in 3rd ch from hook. Fasten off. Sew a small red bead for each eye to front of spider. Attach spider to any part of web.

Legs

Using 3 strands of black embroidery thread, embroider 8 legs. Work a french knot at the end of each leg for the feet.

LADYBIRD

Body

With 4.00mm hook and red yarn, make 3ch, tr6tog in 3rd ch from hook. Fasten off. With 3 strands of black embroidery thread, embroider 'spots' on back of body, by working french knots.

Head.

With 4mm hook and black yarn, make 2ch, 3dc 1ss in 2nd ch from hook. Sew head to one end of the body. Attach 2 small beads for eyes. Sew ladybird to branch of tree on left front.

BEE

Body

With 4.50mm hook and black yarn, make 3ch, tr8tog in 3rd ch from hook. Fasten off. With 3 strands of yellow embroidery thread, embroider two stripes around the body.

Wings

Using 2 strands of gold metallic thread make 'loops' at each side of the bee body. Embroider 2 french knots for eyes before fastening off. Attach a bee to a flower.

FLOWER [Make any number desired]

With 4.00mm hook and orange yarn make 4ch, join with ss to form a ring.

Rnd 1: 1ch, (dc in ring, 2ch)5 times. Join with a ss into top of first st of round. Fasten off orange. Do not turn.

Rnd 3 Join yellow to any 2chsp and work 1dc 2tr 1dtr 2tr 1dc into each 2chsp. Join with ss into top of first dc of rnd. Fasten off.

Attach flowers to jacket, grouping with 2 or 3 leaves.

BRANCHES

Left Front Branch (with monkey): With 4.50mm hook and brown yarn to match front bands, commence at base of branch: 30ch, ss in 2nd ch from hook, 4ss, 8ch, ss in 2nd ch from hook, 3ss,2ch, ss in 2nd ch from hook, 10ss, 5ch, ss in 2nd ch from hook, 12ss, 2ch,ss in 2nd ch from hook, ss in each ch to end. Fasten off.

Sew base of branch to edge of left front band. approx 2.5cm[1in] down from neck edge.

Wrap and curl the monkeys tail around branch and sew in position. Place a few sts in the rem of the branch to secure in place.

Right Front Branch With 4.50mm hook and brown yarn to match front bands commence at base of branch: 30ch, ss in 2nd ch from hook, 11ss, 4ch, ss in 2nd ch from hook, 7ss, 10ch, ss into 2nd ch from hook, 4ss, 4ch, ss in 2nd ch from hook, 12ss, 2ch, ss in 2nd ch from hook and each ch to end. Fasten off.

Sew to right front, positioning base of branch approx 1.25cm[½in] down from neck edge and arrange branches around flowers. Sew in place.

MEDIUM LEAF [for trees etc- approx 11]. With 4.00mm hook and green yarn, make 6ch, ss in 2nd ch from hook, 1dc, 2htr in next ch, 1dc, [1ss, 2ch, 1ss in 2nd ch from hook, 1ss] all in next st. Do not turn, but cont to work along other edge of base ch, 1dc in next ch, 2htr,1dc, 1dc 1ss in last ch. Fasten off.

Sew approx 5 leaves to branch on right front and the rem in groups with the flowers.

LARGE LEAF [foliage - approx 4]. With 4.50mm hook and green yarn, make 9ch, 1ss in 2nd ch from hook, 2dc, 2htr, 2tr, 5tr in next ch. Do not turn but cont to work along other edge of base ch, 2tr, 2htr, 1dc 1ss in next ch. Fasten off.

Sew leaves in pairs to the right front pocket opening and 2 more to the back. Snails or other 'bugs' can be stitched to these leaves.

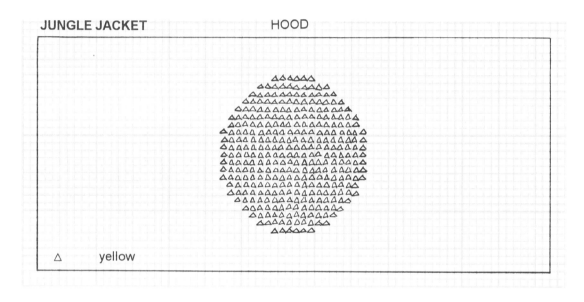

JUNGLE JACKET   **HOOD**

△   yellow

SPIDERS WEB
[worked in silver metallic thread]

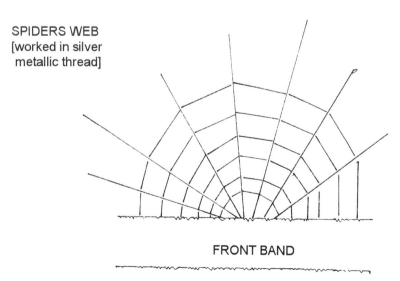

FRONT BAND

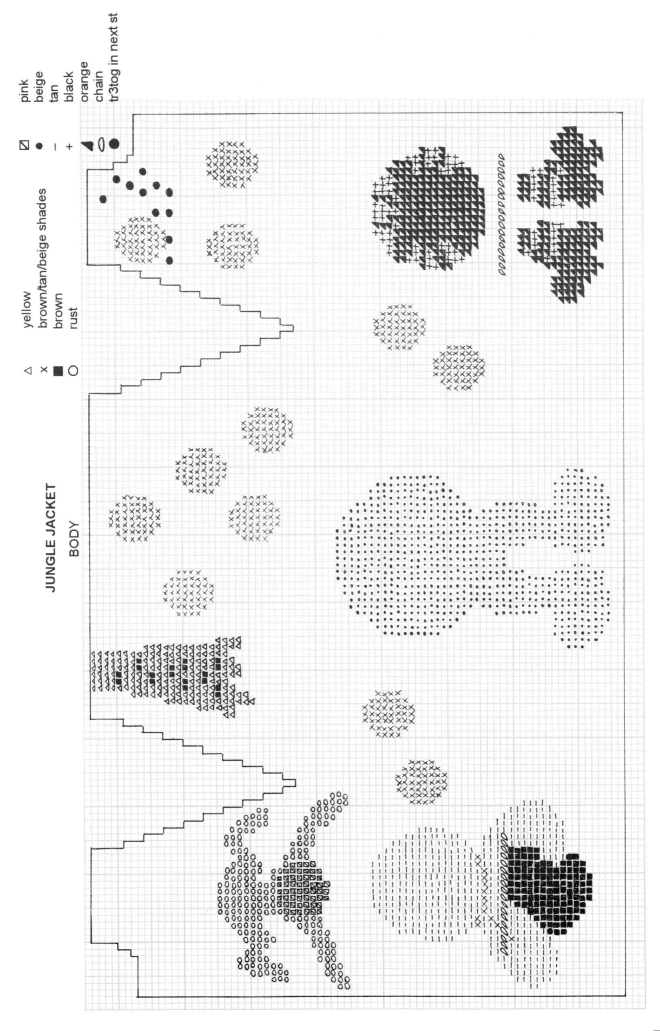

JUNGLE JACKET
BODY

pink
beige
tan
black
orange
chain
tr3tog in next st

yellow
brown/tan/beige shades
brown
rust

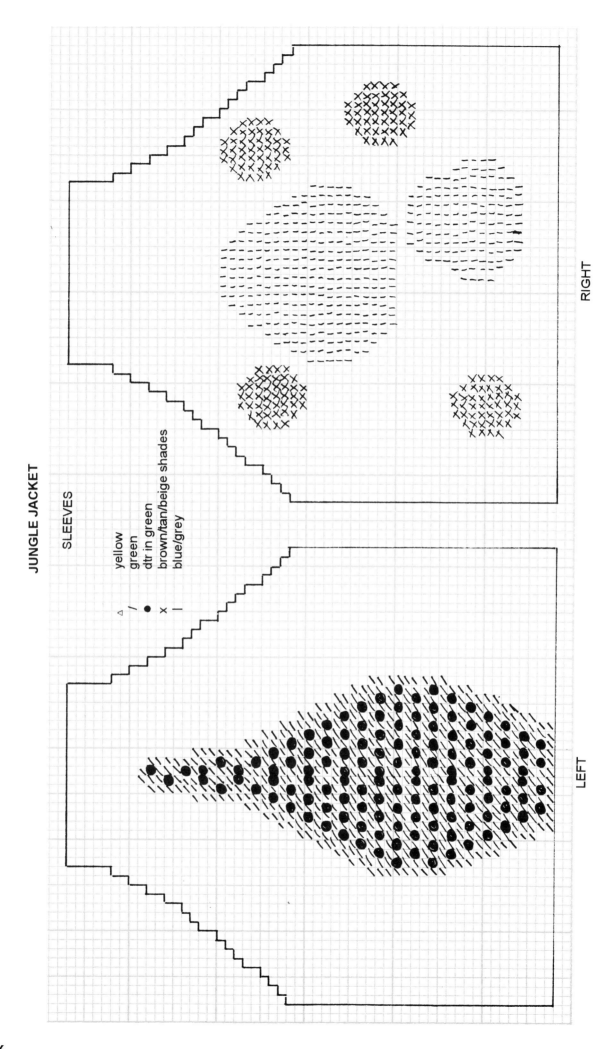

JUNGLE JACKET

SLEEVES

△		yellow
	/	green
●		dtr in green
×		brown/tan/beige shades
	∣	blue/grey

LEFT

RIGHT

ABBREVIATIONS

English terminology has been used throughout. The right hand column gives a US conversion of the stitches where applicable

NB: All asterisked abbreviations have an explanation given in the Techniques Section

English		US TERMINOLOGY	
B*	Bobble		
beg	begin(ning)		
bet	between		
C	contrast colour		
ch	chain		
chsp	chain space		
cl*	cluster		
cm	centimetre		
cont	continue		
CV*	Cable 'V'		
dc	double crochet	sc	single crochet
dc2tog*	decrease 1 dc over 2 sts	sc2tog	dec 1 sc over 2 sts
DDK	double double knitting		
dec	decrease		
dia	diameter		
DK	double knitting		
dtr	double treble	tr	treble
g	gramme		
gr	group	hdc	half double crochet
htr	half treble		
in	inch		
inc	increase		
incl	include		
lp(s)	loop(s)		
M	main colour		
mm	millimetre		
p*	picot		
P*	Popcorn		
patt	pattern		
quadtr	quadruple treble	trtr	triple treble
RdtrF	raised double treble front	RtrF	raised treble front
rem	remaining		
rep	repeat		
rnd(s)	round(s)		
RquadtrF	raised quadruple treble front	RtrtrF	raised triple treble front
RS	right side		
Rtr*	raised treble	Rdc	raised double crochet
RtrB	raised treble pushing stems away from front	RdcB	raised double crochet back
RtrF	raised treble pushing stems to front	RdcF	raised double crochet front
RtrtrF	raised triple treble front		
Rtr2tog	treble 2 raised stitches together		
sdc*	shallow double crochet		
sdc2tog	shallow double crochet 2 stitches together		
sp	space		
ss	slip stitch	slst	slip stitch
st(s)	stitch(es)		
3trcl	3 unfinished trebles worked in one stitch	3dccl	3 dc cluster
4trcl	4 unfinished trebles worked in one stitch	4dccl	4 dc cluster
tog	together		
tr	treble	dc	double treble
tr2tog	decrease 1 tr over 2 sts	dc2tog	dec 1 dc over 2 sts
trtr	triple treble	dtr	double treble
V*	dc spike		sc spike
WS	wrong side		
yoh	yarn over hook		

TECHNIQUES

Slip Knot

a] Wrap the end of the yarn over a circle made from the main ball. Basically you are doing an ordinary slip knot with the main yarn in the left hand and the end of the yarn in the right [assuming you are right handed]. Allow the end of the yarn to be approximately 5cm long.

b] Insert the hook under the back thread from right to left and at the same time make sure the hook is lying over both edges of the circle.

c] Hold the main yarn and the tail end of the yarn and pull the hook up to tighten the loop. Now pull the tail end of the yarn to allow it to hug the circumference of the hook exactly.

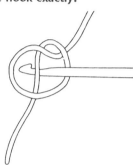

1B = 1 Bobble,

tr5tog on a WS row. This is a like a giant cluster. All stitches are worked in the same place (yoh, insert hook into st, yoh, pull through 2 lps, *yoh, insert hook into same st, yoh, pull through to front, yoh, pull through 2 lps, rep from *three times) 6 lps on hook, yoh, pull through rem 6 lps.

Cl = Cluster,

Work a tr until 2 lps are left on the hook; work another tr in the same place until 3 lps are left on the hook; work a 3rd tr still in the same st until 4 lps are left on the hook, yoh, and draw through all 4 lps.

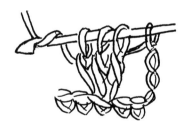

1CV = Cable 'V'

Worked over 5sts on a RS row . Miss next st, 2RdtrFtog worked around stem of tr, 4sts to left of bobble on previous 2 rows, 3tr, 2RdtrFtog around same st, miss next st.

Crab stitch

Insert the hook in next stitch on the right, picking up 2 strands of yarn as normal. Collect the yarn from the ball by dropping the hook head onto the thread as shown in diagram. Bring thread through to the front of

the work making sure there are two loops on the hook. Twist hook to a normal working position, yoh, draw through the 2 loops - one Crab stitch made.

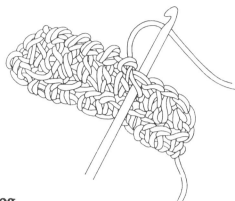

dc2tog

This forms a decrease, *insert hook into next st and draw loop through,rep from * once, yoh and draw through 3 loops on hook.

Picot

1dc, 3ch, ss into 3rd ch from hook

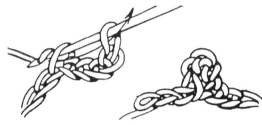

Popcorn

Popcorns can be any number of trebles in one stitch but 4 trebles have been used in this book. Work 4tr in one st, remove hook from last loop and insert hook into top loop of first tr in group, pick up dropped loop and pull loop through, 1ch.

RtrF = raised treble front

Only 2ch to turn is required as the hook is placed into the work around the stem of the stitch and not in the top. Yarn over hook, insert hook from right to left round stem of st, yoh, draw hook from behind stem (3 loops now on hook), *yoh, draw through 2 lps, rep from * once. This stitch raises the treble and pushes it to the front.

RtrB = raised treble back
Work as for RtrF but insert the hook from right to left round stem of st at back of work as shown. The stitch will be pushed to the back of the work.

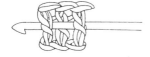

sdc = shallow double crochet
worked as basic dc but on 2nd and subsequent rows insert the hook low into stitch between 2 vertical strands of yarn and below all horizontal strands.

Following charts in sdc
When working colour changes in shallow dc from the chart, read the odd numbered rows from right to left. When working even numbered rows, the turning ch at the beginning of the row counts as the first st. In effect you 'gain' a stitch on these rows but this ensures the pattern works out correctly.

1 TWIST = Crossed raised dtrs
This is worked over 4sts on a RS row. Miss 2sts, 2RdtrF,2RdtrF of 2 missed sts - going in front of last 2sts.

Twisted cord
Cut a length of yarn approximately 4 times the length required and make a loop in both ends. Place one loop around a hook or a small door knob, placing the other loop around your finger, then twist the yarn clockwise keeping it taut. When the twist of the yarn tightens, fold the length in half and the yarn will twist together making a double thickness of twisted cord. Knot the end securely.

V = dc spike,
This is indicated by a 'V' on the chart. The dc spike is worked as an ordinary dc inserting the hook 2 rows below. The yarn should be looped up to lie flat on both sides of the work but without being slack. A slack loop will catch in wear and a tight loop will pucker the main fabric being made.

EYE TEMPLATES

Use any fine see-through paper and with a soft lead pencil [to avoid marking the book] trace the eyes. If you find the soft paper difficult to handle on the felt turn the tracing over and rub the back with the soft lead pencil. Put the rubbing onto a piece of card leaving the clear tracing on top. Retrace over the drawing and cut out the card.

Lion eyes (cut 1 pair)

Tiger eyes (cut 1 pair)

Bear eyes (cut 1 pair)

Large Elephant eyes (cut 1 pair)

Small Elephant eyes (cut 1 pair)

Monkey eyes (cut 1 pair)

HELPFUL TIPS

Colour change
When changing colour work the stitch *before the change of colour* until two loops are left on the hook. Bring the new colour in to finish this stitch to avoid a colour drag.

Colour fast

Children are children, and inevitably the garments being made will need to be washed. If you are in any doubt at all about the fastness of the colour in the yarn being used, try the following test before working the garment.

Wet a white piece of cotton such as an old handkerchief, place a piece of the yarn to be used on the cloth, fold the cloth over, press down with the hand and leave for at least an hour. Press with a warm iron. Look to see if any colour has gone onto the white cloth.

Tension

The designs in this book have been chosen using yarns that are readily available in the shops. Many manufacturers produce DK yarn, however the exact thickness differs from manufacturer to manufacturer.

It is very important a tension swatch is made with the chosen yarn. Adjust the hook if necessary using a larger hook if the tension works out too small and a smaller hook if the tension works out too large. If a DK yarn is specified and a DK yarn is bought, any adjustment should be only one hook size difference. If the hook is changed and more hooks are required please remember to change all the hook sizes either up or down, accordingly.

When measuring the tension, smooth the yarn from the base to the top, and not side to side. Crochet garments hang from the shoulders down. All tensions should therefore be measured after being smoothed in that direction. This will avoid the completed garment becoming too narrow and too long.

Highlighting the eyes

You will see the eyes on the template have a white speck. An embroidered french knot or similar will stop the eyes of the animal from having a "blind look".

Fastening off

After the final stitch has been worked, break the yarn from the main ball leaving approximagely 15cm (6in), or more if you wish to use the yarn to complete a join or add a feature. Work 1ch with this piece of yarn but continue to pull it straight through the loop so that a little knot is formed. Slide the finger and thumb down so that the knot tightens close to the work.

Hook Insertion

Remember to insert the hook under two threads at all times unless otherwise instructed. [eg. sdc picks up three threads, raised stitches go round stems, much of the ribbing picks up only one strand of the stitch]

CONVERSIONS

YARN

Most of the yarn used in these patterns is DK[double knitting], this is equivalent to the US popular sport weight. Aran thickness will work up quite well with a US worsted weight yarn. Chunky yarn will work up well in a US heavyweight knitting worsted weight yarn. If in doubt, check the hook size. All yarns use a regular size of hook for the yarn chosen.

CROCHET HOOKS

HOOK SIZES

U.S.	1/B	2/C	3/D	4/E	5/F	6/G	8/H	9/I	10/J	11/K
Old English	12	11	10	9	8	7	6	5	4	2
Metric	2.25	2.75	3.25	3.5	3.75	4.25	5	5.5	6	7